ANFIELD
VOICES

Liverpool team photograph, 1913/1914 season.

ANFIELD VOICES

DAVID PAUL

AMBERLEY

For the supporters who can no longer go to the game
– especially Ron Hale and George Payne.

First published 1998

Amberley Publishing Plc
Cirencester Road, Chalford,
Stroud, Gloucestershire, GL6 8PE

www.amberleybooks.com

British Library Cataloguing in Publication Data.
A catalogue record for this book is available from the British Library.

ISBN 978-1-4456-0117-5

Typesetting and Origination by Amberley Publishing.
Printed in Great Britain.

CONTENTS

Ness Shankly, Tommy Smith, Bill Shankly and Ray Clemence greet the fans from the balcony outside the Picton Reference Library, the day after winning the FA Cup in 1974.

ACKNOWLEDGEMENTS

Without the generous help of so many people, this collection of stories and photographs would not have been possible. I am especially grateful to Clive and Gill Turner, Ronnie Bracegirdle, Keith Corcoran, Paul Stewart, Jeff Tinnion, Brian Hall (Public Relations Officer at Liverpool Football Club) and Harold S. Scott – a friend of mine and a lifelong Liverpool supporter. I am honoured by, and indebted to, Mrs Ness Shankly for contributing the foreword.

Many other people gave me continued assistance, support and guidance, for which I am most grateful. In particular I would like to thank all the supporters who shared their memories with me and loaned their treasured photographs and other mementoes for inclusion in this book: Mr Arnell, James Bennett, David Boyes, Sharon Bracegirdle, Heather Burke, Trevor Burke, Marilyn Clay, Colette Corcoran, Jason 'JC' Crewe, Ken Davies, Chris Dennis, Ian Durant, Jo Farrell, David Grooby, Mark Howard, Flo Johnston, David Lennon, Jack London, Ivy May, Peter May, Frank McCormack, Paul McEvoy, Craig McGlasson, Kevin Moran, Peter Moran, Peter Moss, Syd Mumford, Terry Murphy, Angela Parry, Paul Parry, Jon Paul, Rene Payne, David Pennington, Sheila Ramsey, Alan Reason, Mark Rochford, Tim Rutter, Don Smith, Margo Stewart, David Stowell, George 'Bob' Stowell, Joe Sullivan, John Sutherland, June Titherington, Gerry Tyrrell and Sam Weston.

Finally, whilst I have tried to ensure that the stories are factually correct (a daunting task in itself), any errors or inaccuracies are mine alone.

FOREWORD

Liverpool Football Club has played a big part in my life for more years than I care to remember now. It was 1959 when Bill became manager at Liverpool and so much has happened since then. Reading the stories in Anfield Voices brings back so many happy memories. The book starts a few years before Bill arrived at Anfield and recounts stories about some of Liverpool's illustrious players of bygone days. I also enjoyed reading about the lengths to which Liverpool supporters will go just to see their team – a passion for football and Liverpool Football Club which I know was shared by Bill. I was also very proud to read the stories about Bill and to know that he still holds a very special place in the memories of so many supporters.

Liverpool is truly one of the greatest football teams, with a long history at the very highest levels of the game. The emphasis has always been on teamwork and I know that this tradition is still at the heart of Liverpool's philosophy and approach, even now. Bill always thought of the supporters as an integral part of the wider team, so I was very pleased when I noticed that the book is dedicated to 'the supporters who can no longer go to the game'.

By Ness Shankly

Ness Shankly

INTRODUCTION

'Some people believe football is a matter of life and death. I am very disappointed with that attitude. I can assure you it is much, much more important than that.'

Bill Shankly
Manager of Liverpool Football Club (1959-1974)

Just as there are many thousands of supporters of Liverpool Football Club from many different walks of life, there is at least an equal number of tales told by those supporters – some happy, some funny, others quite simply bizarre, and, regrettably, some very sad. The volume of statistics goes back as far as 1892, when the club was founded, and it would be a brave person who tried to write a definitive history of Liverpool Football Club. This book is in no way an attempt to do that, instead it is the ordinary fans and their stories that feature in the following pages. Some stories are about players, some about exciting games and some about the weird and wonderful ways in which fans overcame seemingly insurmountable problems to see their glorious team.

Tales of travelling to European ties are in amongst these pages, as are many personal anecdotes from fans who tell how Liverpool Football Club has played a part in their lives. And, because so many people just had to talk about him, a whole chapter is devoted to stories about the great Bill Shankly.

Merseyside has a proud sporting heritage, with football taking pride of place. On any day of the week, conversation in pubs and clubs invariably gets around to football once politics has been cleared out of the way! Liverpudlians have a deep love of the game and many claim to have grown up in either a mixed family or a mixed marriage. This statement doesn't relate to race or religion, but to peoples' allegiance to the Merseyside football teams. Having said that, there is often heard around the city the words of that most famous of all football managers, 'There's two great sides in Liverpool – Liverpool and, er ... Liverpool Reserves'.

All of the photographs and other items of memorabilia in this book have been loaned by the fans themselves. The all-pervading theme of this oral history is the passion and loyalty which Liverpool fans have for their team. Many of the older supporters can no longer attend the games, but their love for Liverpool is just as strong and vivid as when they were young boys standing on the Kop.

The Kop itself is now very different from the way it used to be and the Centenary and Anfield Road Stands have also seen extensive re-development, and no doubt there are more changes planned for the future. Amid all of these changes however, one aspect remains constant – and always will – the indefatigable spirit of the club and its supporters.

David Paul
Liverpool, June 2010

CHAPTER 1

AROUND ANFIELD

It's a Very Emotional Moment

We've had season tickets at Anfield for almost forty years now and don't miss that many games. The seats we have, which have always been the same ones, are halfway up the main stand on the eighteen-yard line near to the Kop end, an ideal vantage point. Even now, after forty years, when just before the game starts and we sing 'You'll never walk alone', and scarves and banners are to be seen all around the ground, there's still a lump comes in my throat; it's a very emotional moment.

James Bennett

My First Game – Fifty Years Ago!

My first Liverpool match, ever, was when we played Grimsby Town in the 1947-1948 season. I was only six at the time, but I still remember that we won 3-1. It's a game that I'll never forget – how could I? It was the last season that Grimsby were in the First Division. They had a goalkeeper named George Tweedy, who was famous for his jersey. It was reputed that he'd worn the same jersey in every match for seventeen years. That was the very first match that my brothers took me. Ironically, both my Grandfather and Father were fanatical Evertonians, but me and my seven brothers all followed the Reds – every single one! Needless to say, football rivalries being what they are in the city, neither my Dad or my Grandfather would ever set foot inside of Anfield – never!

Gerry Tyrell

The 'Paper-Thin' Kop

The Kop's amazing. Over the years it's been extended, taken a bit further back, with new staircases put in – we even had two restaurants built right at the very top. Because of the lack of space, we couldn't have any lifts installed. This meant that every single case of beer, every pork pie and every packet of crisps had to be carted up almost two hundred steps. If you can begin to imagine just how much food and drink is consumed in the Kop on matchdays, then that will give you some idea of the logistics of the operation.

Anfield stadium from the air, 1922.

Banner over the Kop at the start of every home game.

Right: Match programme for the last day of the Kop, Saturday 30 April 1994.

Below: Match ticket for the last day of the Kop, Saturday 30 April 1994.

When they took the decision to build the new, all-seated Kop, and the old one was being taken down, it is frightening to recall just what they found. Some of the main girders that had been there since the stand was built were paper-thin in parts. It appeared that they hadn't been treated over the years, and they'd gone rotten in the ground. Some parts collapsed into a big hole. I didn't actually see it myself, but everyone around the ground was talking about it, and the architects actually took photographs of the state of disrepair. I looked at them, big girders eaten away by rust. I'm sure it was only pressure holding them up. It was the same at the Anfield Road end. When they took the side off it was all tin, the old stand. There were big wooden beams, sunk in places where beams joined, and damp had got in over the years, I suppose they were rotten. It was just pressure holding the damn things up!

Ken Davies

St George at the Kop

Another stupid incident with our Sean: we were in town, I can't remember what particular game it was, but I was about sixteen or seventeen at the time, and we were walking past the Liver Buildings. At the time, the outsides of the buildings were being cleaned after years of dirt and grime had accumulated on the exterior walls. Anyway, halfway up the walls there was a series of flagpoles. On one of them there was the flag of St George proudly flying. All of a sudden our Sean said, 'Just look at the size of that. Imagine getting that and taking it to the Kop!' I suggested that there was no way in which he could possibly climb up the scaffolding on the outside of the buildings – but I was proved to be wrong. The next minute, with the help of a few pints down him, Sean started to make his way up the outside of the building, climbing from one level to the next. His ascent was somewhat precarious, but he eventually did make it, lifted the flag, and then came scampering down much faster than he had got up. We folded the flag and put it away in our workbag. Later that night, the flag was unfurled for the first time on the Kop. After that we used to take that flag to every home game. It's often been seen when the camera has panned around the Kop on Match of the Day.

Mark Rochford

Canteen Development

Well, for me as a caterer it couldn't have been more simple, because nobody in the ground appeared to be at all interested in catering. All they had when I went to Anfield was a couple of shacks dotted in each of the corners and they had a couple of dozen girls working in them. There was only buttons being turned over.

Having been brought up in Canada it was obvious to me, having had some experience of the big stadiums over there, that there was a fortune to be made in catering. Nobody seemed to have grasped this fact, even the directors. They didn't want to run the ground as a business – after all, they were only part time. They all had their own businesses. Most of the directors appeared to be only interested in the

An advertisement for Bovril from a
matchday programme.

football, and of course being directors of the club. As soon as the match was over
they'd leave and wouldn't be seen back at the ground again until the next match. When
I asked for improvements to be made to the catering facilities, nobody would pay any
attention to me. In the end, in desperation, I just went ahead and did it myself! There
seemed to be so much reluctance and, on occasions, positive hostility to development. I
wanted a big canteen to be built near to the flagpole, but the only reaction which I got
was some directors saying, 'Oh no, you won't get one there, you'll never get planning
permission for that.' So I went down to the council, saw the people, got the planning
permission, and then employed a small firm to draw up a canteen facility, cantilevered
over the main passageway under the stand. When it was built it was taking between
£500 and £600 per match, and in catering, with the mark-ups that we make, this was
quite significant, so the next thing I did was to take every available nook and corner
to set up some sort of catering outlet. As I said, when I went to Anfield we had four
shacks, when I left there were some twenty-eight public canteens, all serving a range of
drinks: tea, coffee, chocolate, in addition to a range of beers and soft drinks. We also
sell food, and the turnover is colossal. When I left some two years ago, I was employing
some 200 staff. It has to be said, of course, that John Moores gave me a fairly free hand
to make whatever improvements to catering that I thought were necessary.

Ken Davies

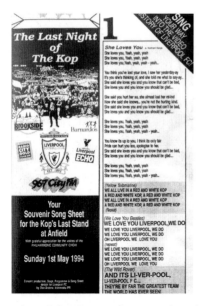

Above left: The souvenir song sheet for the Kop's last stand at Anfield, Sunday 1 May 1994.

Above right: 'Scouser Tommy' – always heard at Anfield, but also at every other venue where Liverpool play.

The 'Specials' from Garston

Going to the match has changed a lot over the years. When I lived in Speke, and times were hard, we'd get the bus from Speke and there'd be a 'special' from Garston.

The bus left at one o'clock on Saturday and it took you to Lake Street – that name will always stick in my memory. There were rows and rows of corporation buses along Lake Street. We'd be dropped off at half past one, and then there'd be the long queue to get in. On the way there, the tickets were thoroughly checked, but on the way back was a very different matter – nobody ever checked the tickets back, so the buses were well over their carrying capacity, but nobody seemed to mind. When we got off at Garston, we were often faced with the three mile walk back to Speke if we'd spent all of our money. It's all changed now, everybody's got cars. I don't think that there are any special buses from anywhere now. The facilities at the ground are also improving. At one time it was a Sayers meat and potato pie, but now you can eat whatever takes your fancy, or whatever your pocket can afford.

In the old days, men used to go to the match wearing a suit, and everybody smoked cigarettes or a pipe. The amount of smoke that could be seen rising from Anfield on a Saturday afternoon was incredible.

Paul Parry

Liverpool against Stoke, early 1970s.

Underneath the Arches

I was on the Kop one day in 1984. I was in my usual spot, and the game was well underway. Towards the front of the stand I could see three girls, aged about twenty, obviously enjoying the game. Five minutes later there was nearly a goal at our end. Whenever this happened, everyone automatically surged forward and today was just the same. When everything has calmed down again – we didn't score – the three girls turned sideways, bent over, and, putting their arms on the shoulders of the girl in front, started to sing the Flanagan and Allen song Underneath the Arches. That still stands out as one of the strangest spectacles I've ever witnessed in years of going to the Kop – it was just so bizarre and spontaneous.

Kevin Moran

Granddad's Broken Arm

We were playing Inter Milan at Anfield. I'd gone along with my Uncle Jack and my granddad. The game was going well, and sometime before half-time we scored. Now, there was a series of steel fences strategically placed all over the Kop at the time – it was part of the crowd control system.

Granddad had his arms hooked over the back of one of these barriers, so that he wouldn't be moved from his preferred spec. But, when the goal was scored, the crowd surged forwards, and Granddad's arm just snapped like a dry twig. There was nothing for it, but to have him lifted up and, unceremoniously, passed over the heads of the fans down to the front where he would be able to receive some medical attention. The last we saw was his little old body being passed over the top. It was just like a human conveyor belt. We settled back to watch the end of the first half. At half-time there was an announcement over the Tannoy system, asking the people who were with Granddad to make their way to the local hospital where they would find him in the casualty ward. Uncle Jack's response was quite unequivocal – 'He'll be alright until the end of the game we've paid good money for these tickets!'

Keith Corcoran

George's Whisky

Whenever there was a home game, George went along and took up his usual seat in the old Kemlyn Road Stand. He'd watched Liverpool for years from the same vantage point: Row C, seat No. 72. During the game, he'd also enjoy the odd slug of White Horse whisky, taken from his hip flask. He always drank White Horse. The chap next to him happened to be a Bells employee and became a little disturbed when George told him that he was drinking White Horse. As some sort of incentive, or even a little gift, this chap said that if George changed to Bells in his hip flask, then he would reward him with a bottle of whisky. When the next game came along, George had long forgotten about this conversation, and duly took along his White Horse. Halfway through the game, the chap next door asked if George had changed his allegiance. George said that of course he had. Just to check it out, the guy next door had a sip of George's whisky and when he had satisfied himself that it was indeed Bells, he rewarded George with his promised bottle of whisky. George was very late home that night, and a little the worse for the experience!

Rene Payne

The Roar of Anfield

We used to live about a mile from the ground and, in those days, Liverpool used to get over 50,000 for the most innocuous League game. Sometimes, when we were sat at home, all we could hear was these shouts and roars and I wondered 'What's going on down there?' My next thought was 'I might go to see them sometime'. I can't actually remember who it was against when I went to my first game, as I'd only be about six – that would be in 1958. I got really interested in it when I was about eleven years old, something like that. Of course, things really took off for me in 1959, when Shankly came to Liverpool.

David Pennington

It's Got to Be the Chippy First

What upsets me at the moment, is the way that the game's being taken away from the ordinary working man. I used to work overtime and workmates would say, 'Are you going to the match tonight?' and we'd rush out in overalls, nip into a fish and chip shop, and either have a pie and chips or fish and chips, and then it was off to the match. It was half a crown in those days. In the Kop, there was a broken loudspeaker – Liverpool must have had one of the worst loudspeaker systems in the country – and we used to meet directly under this speaker. We used to travel all over the country. It's not quite the same today, the accent's on money, and there's lots of greed in the game. It's not as honest as it used to be.

Peter May

The 'Vomitory'

We got a couple of tickets when the new Centenary Stand was built. Entering for the first time and rising up through the beautifully appointed Paisley and Shankly Lounges to the Premier Club, I was really impressed with the quality of the fittings and the state of execution of the job. Arriving on the main entrance area where the toilets were and whatever, and looking for ways of getting into the stand area, I found that some bright spark, looking for an appropriate title for the passageway into and out of the crowd area, had used a term of 'Vomitory' to describe the egress. Needless to say, 'Vomitory' and Scouse humour went down extremely well, but before the next match, 'Vomitory' had been changed to something far more respectable like 'Entrance' or something like that. I don't know if this was a simple sort of an admin blunder or maybe it was just a marketing gaff.

Heather Burke

Falling Down the Kop Steps

I started going to Liverpool matches on a regular basis when it was nine pence, old money, to go in the boys' pen up at the top corner. Once inside, it was up and over the wall, then over the railings, and finally back down and you were now in the two shilling Kop! If you wanted, from the Kop you could go to the Paddock, but in the Kop you had complete freedom of movement. I was about four foot eight at that time, and I couldn't climb up half of the time, but nonetheless, it was over the railings and into the Kop. I recall coming out of the ground one day with a friend of mine, who promptly fell down all of the steps at the back of the Kop – right from the top to the bottom – all the way. My friend must have been over six foot tall, and I carried him all the way home from the ground to Edge Hill. It took us about three hours, but he'd broken his ankle as he fell. His mum and my mother were friends. He was an only child and he got away with murder – he really did get away with murder. Whenever we did anything wrong, he took a great delight in telling his mother, who promptly told my mother, who promptly larruped me. Some thanks!

Alan Reason

Fainting in the Kop

When we went into the Kop, we used to queue up for ages, and eventually got in about an hour and a half before the start of the game. The idea was to get exactly the spec that we wanted, usually halfway up the Kop towards the middle of the stand. This was the place that just about everyone else wanted as well. As the Kop began to fill up, we got a little more squashed, and maybe moved to one side a little, until by the time it got to kick-off, we were nowhere near where we had started. It didn't make that much difference, as we didn't see that much of the game anyway. One of our taller friends expressed an interest in coming along to the matches. We thought that this was a splendid idea, as he'd be able to shield us from the crowds. The reverse was true. Shortly after the game started, he was so crushed that he just fainted. There was nothing for it, but to pass him over the heads of the crowd, as was the usual practice then – and still is today for that matter. We carried on watching the match and didn't see him, or the friend who'd gone with him, until after the game. As we were on the train going home they told us what a fantastic afternoon they'd had. The first aid room was located near to the players' entrance and, after our friend had recovered, he'd sat watching the match from that superb vantage point. To add insult to injury, he'd also been plied with copious mugs of hot tea throughout the duration of the game just to make sure that his strength was returning. One or two of our friends tried the same dodge in subsequent weeks, but we were soon 'rumbled'.

Tim Rutter

The Wrigley's Chewy Sellers

There were guys who walked around the ground before the matches and also at half-time. They wore official red jackets with, I think, 'Wrigley's' written on the back. Around their necks they carried big trays. They were, for all the world, just like the usherettes in cinemas. On the trays they had Wrigley's chewing gum, Mars bars, Opal Fruits and other assorted sweets and goodies. Fans threw their money on to the pitch and shouted down which particular item they wanted. After checking that they'd received the correct money, the sellers would then select the appropriate piece of confectionery and hurl it towards the crowd. They were so skilled, just like darts players, that everyone always received what they'd asked for. If, by any chance they missed, people would pass on the sweets to the chap who had paid for them.

Paul McEvoy

Can I Mind Your Bike Please?

When I was a very young boy growing up in Liverpool, which is now many more years ago than I care to remember, my gran lived in Venmore Street. Now, Venmore Street is not too far from Liverpool's ground. So, when there was a home match, and with Gran's permission, I'd wait by the ground for the supporters who arrived at the game on

A scene from a Varthen
Street celebration.

their bikes. Many of them would have cycled straight from work in order to get to the
match on time. For the princely sum of sixpence, I used to relieve them of their mounts
at the ground entrance and issue them with a cloakroom ticket. The tickets had Gran's
address on the back, so, when the game was over, they walked through the jiggers and
collected their bikes. Of course, in those days every one was very trustworthy and there
was no danger of you running off with their bikes. As the seasons went by, this little
enterprise became a regular and very profitable source of income.

Mr Arnall

The Ashes Must Have Helped

In the November of 1995 we were going through a bad spell – we hadn't won a
game for ages. It was so bad in fact that some fans were beginning to call it 'Black
November'. I thought that it was a particularly black month anyway, as my stepfather,
a true 'Red' since his childhood, also died. George's wish was to have his ashes
scattered over Anfield. We contacted Mrs Walsh – Roy Evan's secretary – as you've
got to get permission from the club before you're allowed to do anything like that.
Anyway, permission was given and when we got to the ground we were greeted by the
groundsman, Reg.

Above left and right: Whenever Liverpool won anything, even if it was just an important league game, there was always a party in Varthen Street.

Just another queue on Saturday afternoon.

We all went along, Mum, Colette, one of George's great friends, Tommy Whiteside, and myself. We went up to George's old seat C72. The idea was to spread the ashes near there. As we were making our way up, I happened to mention to Reg the poor run of form which we were experiencing at the time. Then, inspired, Reg (who happens to be an Evertonian) suggested that we should go down to the Kop goalmouth and spread the ashes there. Our next match was against Man U, and we won 2-0. This was a very promising start! We went on to win a string of matches after that. Say what you like, but Mum insists that the ashes must have had something to do with it!

Keith Corcoran

The Parties in Varthen Street

Every time Liverpool won anything, the League, the FA Cup, the European Cup – anything at all – we would have a street party. The atmosphere was always warm and the parties went on long into the night. We lived in Varthen Street which is just off Walton Breck Road, not so far from the ground.

June Titherington

The Old Man in the Kop

I always remember one guy who used to be in the Kop. Me and our Sean used to go when we were kids and this guy, whose name we never knew, always used to sit somewhere around the right-hand side of the goalpost. We'd get the 78 from the English Rose on Mackets Lane, down as far as Wavertree Road and then we'd either get the 26 or the 27, whichever came first, to take us to Sheil Road. Then, we'd jump off and walk down to Anfield. I always remember standing outside of the ground, thousands of us kids, and the police on their horses towering over us, and you'd always be petrified in case one of the horses bumped into you, because you'd expect that it was going to kick you or something like that. Now and then we used to climb up onto the outside toilets. These toilets were situated just on the corner of the Kop. We used to go in there and then get a 'bunk-up'. As there was no roof on the toilet, once you were over the wall, you were right in the Kop! So most weeks we could get in for free. We always stood in the same place every week, just where this guy used to stand. He'd always have his arms on the bar, and he would chat to us – we were twelve or thirteen at the time and he'd let me and our Sean sit on the bar, while he made sure that we didn't fall off. Even when there was a surge when we looked like scoring a goal, he didn't let us go.

Mark Rochford

All Night Queues

Years ago, well before they had season ticket holders at the club, fans would queue up all night for cup tickets. People were really keen in those days. Tickets were sold on a

Paul Stewart – 'the view from where we sit'.

first-come, first-served basis. The queues used to be right down the side of the park. They'd queue all night, without anything to eat or drink. So I had the idea of bringing in some of the women who worked for me. We found some old trolleys and then made some minor modifications. On the trolleys we had big stainless steel urns full of tea, and hanging down the sides of the trolleys we had bags of crisps. We also used to sell hot meat pies and sausage rolls. When the girls ran out of tea and pies they'd come back, re-fill and go out again. We did a brisk trade, but we were also providing a good and much-needed service.

Ken Davies

More Loos in the Kop

Bill Shankly, as far as I'm concerned, was the man who turned Liverpool around. He built his first team on Yeats, and gradually things got better and better. Everyone's standard of living went up, and so did the money. Once he'd begun to sort the team out, he turned his attention to the ground, which was just as well. At that time, there were very few toilets in the Kop, and of course the whole of the stand was always jam-packed full. So, when people needed to relieve themselves at halftime, they'd often pee into someone else's pocket – not a very nice thing to happen when it happened to you! Fortunately, the new loos which Shankly had built in the Kop changed that particular practice.

Syd Mumford

My Parka Pocket's Wet

One winter, one of the members of our little gang got a new Parka. He was very proud of this new coat, as he was at pains to tell us – whenever the opportunity arose. He'd got the Parka for his birthday the day before, and when he wore it for the match the next day, everyone was quite envious. We went and watched the game and then caught the train home to Runcorn. On the way back, our friend remembered that he had some sweets left in his pocket which he hadn't got round to eating during the afternoon. He put his hand in his pocket and it was wet through and all of the sweets were soggy! The obvious had happened. Somebody had rolled up a newspaper and relieved themselves into his pocket. Our friend wasn't too pleased about this. Worse was to come, he still had his mother to face when he got home. The rest of us, whilst not showing obvious delight, were all secretly thinking that he deserved it anyway!

Tim Rutter

Beaker Beer

Another idea which I had was to sell beer in the ground. It seemed stupid for people to be sitting in pubs and then rushing to get into the ground before kick-off time. I took some guidance, but was advised that it was illegal to sell half pints or pints in the ground. After a considerable amount of research I found out that it was legal to sell beer in measures other than the traditional quantities – I still needed to obtain a drinks license. The cups which the beer was sold in contained about nine fluid ounces – just less than half a pint. A problem then arose – what do we call it? In the end we settled on the title 'Beaker Beer'. We had posters put on all of the walls, 'Beaker Beer – a shilling'. I seem to recall that it sold really well.

Ken Davies

Season Ticket Dodges

They used to have season tickets and you would show it as you walked in – it was just like my bus pass. For some reason, people weren't content with that and they used to bring their children along with them, and pass them over the turnstiles. This was okay when the kids were small, but then the kids grew bigger, and they were still passing them over, even when the youngsters were fifteen and sixteen years old, they'd still be passed over the turnstile. Understandably, people used to complain, because when the kids were small they could sit either side by side or on their dad's knee, but as they got bigger, they often filled the seat next to them as well. There were lots of arguments about this particular dodge. Another trick that was used with season tickets was where somebody would go in with a season ticket and buy a programme. He'd then come back and say to his mate on the other side of the turnstile, 'There's the programme that you wanted', and, of course, what he'd done was to place the season ticket inside the match programme. So two people used to get in for the price of one and they'd stand in the gangways. Yet another trick which was often used was that the ticket was just thrown out past the turnstile and their mates would be waiting outside. Again, two people were getting in for the price of one. Liverpool brought out a system whereby you received a book of tickets and used one ticket for every match. This slowed things down considerably, but it was their own fault. They were cutting off their noses to spite their faces, because, as you know, when the roar goes up as the match starts, everyone wants to be in, but they had to wait while we examined the details on the ticket. When they were late, some fans resorted to taking a run and jump right over the top of the turnstile from way out down the road. But that was Liverpool then, and it was a good atmosphere to work in.

Syd Mumford

Going Home by Tram

In the mid-fifties, Liverpool were still in the old Second Division. We had a match scheduled at Anfield to play Cardiff – they were in the same division. At the time, my cousin, Doreen, was engaged to a Welsh graduate working for Lever Brothers in Bromborough – Bleddyn. As a keen Cardiff supporter, he was anxious to see the match and invited me, a young boy of eleven in my first year at secondary school, to accompany him to the match – I was delighted. Of the few matches that I had been to up until that date, all of them, bar none, were seen from a lowly position in the Kop – I was only just over five feet tall at that time! Today, we were going to have a seat in the Kemlyn Road stand – very expensive! Although I can't claim to remember too much about the game, as I was so excited, I seem to recall that we managed to win. Bleddyn wasn't too happy with this outcome, but I think that he enjoyed the game, as he was full of praise for Liverpool as we made our way to the tram-stop. At the time, I wasn't too sure how to get home to Speke from Anfield, but Bleddyn assured me that the best way, by far, was to catch a tram into the city centre, and then get the 82d from the Pier Head. It wasn't too long before the 'Green Goddess' was approaching our stop. There was always a fascination in travelling upstairs, in fact, children were not allowed upstairs unless accompanied by an adult. The upper deck was reserved for smokers, and as we climbed the winding staircase at the rear of the tram, we were met with a 'fug' of stale Woodbine smoke, mingled with the stale Senior Service smoke from the more affluent passengers. The tram took us to the main terminus at the Pier Head. From there we walked across to the bus-stops – where the tram lines hadn't penetrated. That journey was the last tram journey I went on in Liverpool.

David Paul

CHAPTER 2

TRAVELLING TO GAMES

We Did the Dash from Grange-over-Sands to Anfield in Sixty-One Minutes!

We'd been spending a few days up at Grange-over-Sands, where our family owned a holiday home. On the Saturday morning some friends, who also had a holiday home in the Lakes, came over and we all went for a walk along the Promenade. We then drove to one of our favourite pubs in Lindale for lunch. As the sun was shining we sat outside, ate our lunch and drank the odd pint or two. Just after one-thirty my friend said that he and his son would have to leave, as they were driving down to Anfield for the first game of the season. It was obvious, judging from the faces of my two sons, that they were quite envious. I tentatively asked if there was any possibility of getting a few tickets for the Kop, or anywhere else in the ground for that matter. My friend said that he would be able to arrange it. By now it was almost quarter to two, and the game was due to start at three o'clock. We went back to our caravan, had a quick wash and picked up some money, and then we headed off for the M6 and Anfield.

Although normally a law-abiding citizen, on this occasion my friend broke all of the speed limits in his white Saab; at times we reached speeds of over one hundred miles per hour! The three boys sat in the back seat totally mesmerised by the speed and also the prospect of seeing Liverpool play. I think that David was spurred on by their enthusiasm and also the clock which was now inexorably moving closer to three o'clock. We did the dash from Grange-over-Sands to Anfield in sixty-one minutes! Liverpool started the season with a spirited win, which pleased all of us.

Chris Dennis

The Car's on Fire!

We went down to a game against Ipswich. I went along with my wife-to-be, her brother and one of our other mutual friends. Well, we set off, and there were no problems until we got to Rugby and, as we came off the M1, the car, which was a big Volvo, just shuddered to a grinding halt and stopped – it just died! Fortunately, there was a garage not very far away, so we pushed it to there and had a word with the chap who owned the garage. He merely confirmed that our motor had seen its last trip on a motorway – it was a sad moment. We were then a bit stuck. But the gods were with us that day. In

He's always asleep whenever we need to fill up!

the reception room at the garage there was a small TV. My future brother-in-law was a keen gambler, and proceeded to make a phone call to his bookies at home. In less than an hour, we had enough money to hire a car for the remainder of the weekend, and enough left over to ensure that we enjoyed all of the weekend from that point on. Before too long we were off again and speeding towards Ipswich. We got to the ground, won the game, had a few pints and decided to make a good night of it – our money worries now firmly behind us. Shortly after eleven o'clock when we were being ushered out of the pub, we set off for home. We were driving up what I think was the A47, when our driver made a request for us to stop smoking in the back, as he couldn't see out of the rear view mirror. I replied that my girlfriend was asleep, and that I didn't smoke. In the nick of time the car was pulled off the road and burst into flames as we were escaping! The engine, which was at the rear of the car, had gone on fire. It was after three o'clock in the morning before a replacement car arrived. By this time we were cold, wet, tired and hungry, and feeling very, very sorry for ourselves. The Hillman Avenger which arrived just about managed to get us back to the Wirral, but it wasn't the happiest of car journeys. We arrived home at seven o'clock in the morning and two of us had to be in work that day – never again ... until the next time that is!

Paul Stewart

An Exciting Weekend Away

Most of my family went to the match and still do and I used to go with my two cousins Janet and Diane. We would stand in the Paddock next to the trainer's box. We'd go to the ground at eleven o'clock on a Saturday morning, to queue up to get in so that we could get our spec. One Easter, Liverpool were playing Newcastle away and we thought that we would have a trip to Newcastle, as none of us had ever been there before. We thought that we would be better going up on the Good Friday and make a good weekend of it – well, that's what we thought. Janet had a car at that time, so we drove up to Newcastle on the Good Friday and tried to find somewhere to stay – remember, this was about twenty-five years ago. The big hotels were too big and too expensive and small hotels just didn't exist, so we wandered around and we passed a police station – so we went in. We asked was there anywhere in the locality that we could stay for the night we even tried asking if they had an empty cell! They directed us down the road to the YWCA, so we went along and booked in there. Then we went out for a wander around to see what was happening in and around Newcastle on this Good Friday evening, but nothing was happening. In fact, the only sign of life was seeing all of the drunks rolling in the gutters and nothing else at all. To make matters worse, we had to be back in the YWCA at ten o'clock! So, we didn't have an exciting time. We went back to the room. It was a very big room, and we were sharing it for the night. Inside was just like outside – there was nothing happening at all. There was a deafening silence all around, we thought that we were the only ones there until about midnight when there was a hammering on the door, and it was a Chinese girl demanding a pen – or we thought that she wanted a pen. So we eventually decided that, yes, she needed a pen, so we gave her a pen, and off she went. And that was our exciting weekend. We went to the match the next day, and I can't even remember whether we won or not. All we needed to do then was to drive back home on the Saturday night. I don't think that either of us has been to Newcastle since.

Marilyn Clay

The Flat-Bed to Anfield

When I used to go to the game, a million years ago, I had a season ticket for the Kop. There was a big gang of us from Runcorn went along – anything between eight and fifteen guys depending upon who had any money and who didn't. We used to get the train from Runcorn and get off at Edge Hill and then we used to walk the rest of the way to the ground – it was miles away! We took to waiting by traffic lights and when a flat-bed lorry came along, we'd jump on the back and hitch a lift. The drivers never seemed to mind. When they were turning off, they'd give us a signal, and we'd jump off at the next corner. I'm sure that anything like that wouldn't happen today.

Tim Rutter

Phoning In Ill Doesn't Work

My dad worked for a company called Merseyside Metal Windows and he used to go all over the country watching Liverpool play football. I liked the idea of this. It sounded great, going all over the place, having a few beers and seeing an exciting game

Taken from the match programme of
the Liverpool v Leeds United FA Cup
Final, 1965.

of football. Having said that, at the time I was only about nine or ten, so my away
trips would have to wait for a few years. Later in life, I teamed up with a group of
friends, and we've been absolutely everywhere following Liverpool. Not only has it
been exciting, but it's also been quite nerve-wracking on many occasions. More than
once I've nearly lost my job over being away from work and using the flimsy excuse
that I was ill when there was an important European game being played. Although
I've never actually been sacked, I've had final warnings a few times. The real problems
started when Sky TV started panning around the stands, and I've also been seen on
Match of the Day a couple of times.

Paul Stewart

Red Tickets and White Tickets

When we were in the Second Division, for those seven long years, we played many
clubs in Lancashire – Bury, Bolton, Blackburn and teams like that. Because it was
in Lancashire, the train ticket always cost seven-and-six, irrespective of where in
Lancashire the game was being played. It was still seven-and-six, even when we used
to go to Preston. The trains always left from Exchange Station, but on Wednesday
afternoon we had to go down and stand in a queue for the ticket. If you didn't get
your ticket on a Wednesday, then there was no way that you could get to the match.
There weren't very many cars then. When Saturday came, you'd have to queue again
to get on the train, and we were packed in like sardines. They weren't corridor trains,
because it was only a local service. We were always first in the queue to make sure that

we got on the first train. I always liked to be first there, even at that age, fourteen and fifteen. The tickets for train number one were always red, and then train number two would be in white, because Liverpool's away colours were white then. They also had orange, green and yellow tickets. After the game, on the way home, the colour of the ticket didn't count, it was every man for himself. Invariably, just being kids, we used to get pushed to the back. All the men would push us to the back and we'd get one of the later trains, arriving home at all hours of the night. Even though my dad was an Evertonian, and had eight sons, he'd always come down to the station to meet the train. That was every time we went to an away game. There was only one exception to that rule, and that was the day when we beat Everton in the 1950 Cup Semi-final – he wasn't waiting for the train then!

Gerry Tyrell

Getting Locked Up!

The first away game that I went to was against Wolves in the League Cup. Me and our Sean went down to Lime Street Station, got on the train with the other kids and all the rest of the fans. I must have been about thirteen or fourteen at the time; I can't see youngsters of that age today being allowed to go to Wolves on their own. Their parents just wouldn't let them go. When we got there, I remember them scoring. As we got in we were allocated all of the away end and we were stuck in the middle, but the atmosphere was great. I'd already been to Anfield and our Sean had been to Man City and United. He'd been going to matches for a few seasons before me. I was just standing there, absorbing the atmosphere and, before I knew it, I ended up on the pitch. Just that split second and all of a sudden you're on the pitch. You can imagine, there was quite a crush in that stand. I always remember being on the pitch, the referee had blown the whistle, and Kevin Keegan just stopped everyone from celebrating, saying, 'NO, no, it's a free kick, it's not over yet' and the game went on. At the end of the game, all of the Wolves supporters just stood there and they all applauded – everyone was clapping.

Coming home on the train, everyone was switching the lights on and off. We were on one of the 'Specials' and I said to our Sean, 'Don't do that, because there's loads of Transport Police on the train and they're dressed in plain clothes', but Sean, being Sean, wouldn't heed my warning and went on messing about, switching the lights on and off. In desperation I said, 'Sean, you're going to get caught.' The very next minute he switches the lights off again and everyone was saying, 'Who switched the lights off?' – so, as he switched them on again, a chap grabbed hold of him and said, 'That's it, I'm going to arrest you'. So, when we got back to Lime Street and I said to one of these Transport Police, 'My brother's been locked up, can you tell me where he is?' and he said, 'Oh, he'll be up by the mail trains, in the mail carriages.' What they'd done was, they'd locked him into one of the mail carriages. They'd turned around to him and said, 'You're not going anywhere', then they'd opened the cage in the mail carriage, thrown him in and then just locked it. I don't know what happened afterwards, but I think that he was let off with just a telling off. But that day, that game and that event always stick out in my mind.

Mark Rochford

British Rail

On Boxing Day 1962, Liverpool were scheduled to play at Aston Villa. We travelled down by train and, as we pulled into Witton Station, a porter on the platform waved the train straight through, shouting that we should go to Birmingham New Street as the game had been called off.

You may recall that the winter of '62/63 was the winter of the snow and football was all but abandoned for three months. Anyway, we went through to New Street – we weren't even allowed to get off the train. We couldn't go to the toilets and we couldn't get any refreshments. We were kept there for about half an hour or so and then the train pulled out. By now it must have been about two-thirty. We got as far as Crewe and the train stopped again. Bear in mind, the train had no toilets, there were no refreshments, there was no heating and there was no lighting. By this time it was dark, or very close to being dark, and the train remained in the middle of nowhere with a lot of unhappy passengers. Anyway, I eventually got home at about four o'clock in the morning, and it was only then when we found out what had been the problem. On the way home, a train had been derailed outside Crewe blocking the line and holding everyone up. A number of people had been killed and others injured, a fact not communicated to us on the train.

Eventually I arrived home having slid and fallen all the way from the station to home to be greeted by my parents who knew of the derailment but obviously did not know where I was or whether or not our train had been involved. It's when you're cold, tired and hungry, that you start talking about going by car or coach, but not by train. If we had have been on a coach we could at least pulled up somewhere – we couldn't and we didn't.

Alan Reason

Peter Thompson is on the ball against Sheffield United at Bramall Lane.

My Cylinder Head's Gone

I had this old car, an old Morris ten, and a gang of us all got in and went off to Blackburn. On the way, the cylinder head gasket went, but we carried on. It meant stopping every now and again, getting water, and topping the radiator up. Anyway, we got to the match okay. I couldn't tell you what the result of that one was, because I remember the journey more than the match. On the way back, the cylinder head situation was getting worse. It was okay when you were driving along, but when you stopped with the engine just ticking over, there'd be a build up of water getting into the engine – so when you put your foot down, there'd be an almighty cloud of steam coming out, which blotted out everything behind. We came to a policemen on point duty, and we were right at the front of the traffic. There was a coach behind us, and the policeman turned to me and waved me to go forward. I put my foot down, moved forward and there were clouds of steam everywhere – it blotted out the coach behind us and everything. As we went past, the policeman looked aghast, as if to say 'What's going on?' On the way back we decided to have a drink, which was normal in those days with no breathalyser, so we had a drink. We spent the best part of the evening in this old pub between Blackburn and Liverpool. When we came out later, I think that they closed at ten in those days, we got into the car and the battery was flat. So I went and got the starting handle out whilst they were all sitting in the car, and I put the starting handle in the car but I just couldn't turn it. So I said to the others, 'The cylinders have filled up with water, I just can't turn the engine over – give us a hand'. So, a group of them came out and there were about three of us all wrestling with the starting handle, trying to turn it, and I thought that we would have to clear the water, so we started turning the engine over. And then somebody said, 'The car's moving forward'– it was just in gear, that was all that was wrong with it! We were laughing about that all the way home.

Jack London

Holes in My Shoes

I was going to an away game at Sunderland, and had to pick up the coach about a mile and a half from home. I couldn't afford the bus fare to get to the coach and so, lightly clad, with shoes that had just a mere skin on the soles, I set off on the short walk to meet the coach. By the time I got to the pick-up point, a hole was already beginning to form in the sole of the shoe. Fortunately, although the weather was turning bad and it was starting to snow, I managed to get on the coach and join my friends and colleagues. The journey to Sunderland, which was a good six-and-a-half hour drive away at that time, proved to be a great trip. However, when we got there we found that we had tickets for the wrong end – the Sunderland end – and we were treated pretty inhospitably by the Sunderland crowd of steel workers and dockers. They seemed to resent the fact that, in spite of the frozen conditions, Liverpool went one-up pretty quickly. We ended by winning the match 2-1. The game was over, and on a complete cloud, we set off for the coach. All the time the snow was getting thicker and thicker, and it took over eight hours to get back to Speke, with the coach slipping and sliding all over the road. By now, the soles of my shoes had worn considerably more, and the hole, which was maybe the size of a pinhead to start with, was now well over the size of a two pence piece. My socks were torn, my feet were feeling very sore and I was faced with the prospect of having to walk all the way from the roundabout by Evans Medical to my home in Millwood Road. Even then, with the water coming into my feet and the soles of my shoes completely in ribbons, there was no pain – just the exhilaration of victory.

Trevor Burke

A Bentley's the Only Way to Travel

Liam had just bought this big red Bentley with leather seats. They were a sort of a cream colour, which matched the colour of the car to perfection. The car was completely unbelievable – there was a mini bar and a ten-inch TV in the back. I'd never seen a car like it. Anyway, we were scheduled to go to this game against Aston Villa and one of our other friends who worked at the courier company just down the road was going to be our driver for the day and he'd arranged to pick us up at nine o'clock on Saturday morning. The idea was to go down in his car, drive down to a hotel, have some mid-morning breakfast, and then go on to Aston Villa to watch the game. Things didn't work out quite like that. When John saw the car, he was completely thrown. He said that he'd always wanted to drive a car such as that. So, without any second bidding, Liam threw the keys over to him. This was pure fantasy stuff! We drove down the M6 in the beautiful red Bentley. Everyone was looking as we overtook them in the outside lane – I don't think that we dropped below ninety all the way down. As it happens, we won the game, but

Aston Villa Football Club

V.I.P. HOSPITALITY

v

LIVERPOOL

on **SATURDAY 7TH MAY 1994**

Venue **PREMIER CLUB** Villa Park

Arrive **12.15PM PREMIER CARVERY**

A meal will be served before the game

N.B. Car Parking is not available at Villa Park however free parking is available at the nearby Aston Villa Leisure Centre, Aston Hall Road, upon production of this invitation.

STRICTLY NO JEANS, TRACKSUITS OR TRAINERS

The ticket from a very special day out for Paul Stewart at Aston Villa.

the whole experience was completely surreal. When we arrived at the hotel in Walsall, we were treated like royalty or pop stars. They really thought that we were celebrities.

Paul Stewart

Taking the Silver

On the way to a match in Manchester, I stopped for a swift half at the Greyhound, a friendly and well-patronised pub just along the East Lancs Road. Sat over in the corner, I saw two very well known Liverpool players. At the time there was lots of publicity about how Scousers were not very ethical or desirable people. Well, there just happened to be two Scousers who were sat near to the famous duo and they'd decided to pull the respective legs of the players. The line of conversation was focused on some of their play and commitment during recent matches. It was all in a good-natured sort of way. What my fellow Scousers didn't know was that each time they looked from one to the other, or became distracted, one of the players was putting some silverware off an adjacent table into their pockets. Later, as the Scousers were walking away from the table, the players called over the manager of the pub, and told him that these two Scousers were on their way out with their pockets full of silverware. The two guys were apprehended. Later, it was explained that it was only a joke – and it was all taken in good part. But the look on these two young men's faces for taking the mickey out of the Liverpool players had to be seen to be believed.

Trevor Burke

The Match that Cost Me £2,000

I was dashing home from Manchester one night to get to a match. It was a November night and it was pouring with rain. It was as black as Hades and I drove straight into a guy on the M56. I absolutely slammed straight into the back of him. The only thing that I can think of is that I dozed off. Fortunately, I hit him absolutely square, so he didn't get pushed to either side, it was just a straight forward shunt. So we pulled over and I admitted responsibility there was no way I could avoid it. It cost me over two grand to get the car fixed! And I thought to myself, well, you know, at two thousand pounds, I can't afford it. Not only that, I was bloody lucky because the whole of the front of the car had gone, I had no lights, no indicators – nothing, and I managed to drive along the whole of the M56 to get home. Obviously, I missed the match. I then started to ask myself, 'What's the point – if it was me, would they come and see me?' and the obvious answer was 'No'. So, all of a sudden, you begin to fall out of love and then one Saturday afternoon, my girlfriend asked me to take her shopping. I said that there was a match and we began to argue. In the end I said 'Okay, fine, we'll go shopping'. And from that point on we just went shopping on Saturday afternoons. The season ticket came up at the end of the year and I thought, 'Well, I'm not paying £100 for this', as I wasn't going to the games any more, so I just let it lapse.

Alan Reason

CHAPTER 3

THE CUP TRAIL

Wednesday's Woe

I'd just taken a job over in Sheffield and, as it happens, Liverpool were playing in a very important cup game against Sheffield Wednesday later that month. Although I tried all of my usual sources, I couldn't get a ticket for the game. Then, and very unexpectedly, one of my new colleagues, a certain Giles Pepler, said that he could secure a ticket for me – he was an ardent Wednesday supporter. But, there was a downside; he said that I would be next to him in the Leppings Lane end, and that was where many of the Wednesday supporters were. Undeterred, I accepted the ticket and, on the night itself, found myself surrounded by Wednesday supporters. This wasn't too bad, until that is, Liverpool scored. Unconsciously, I jumped up and cheered at the top of my voice, only to be smartly pulled back by Giles! I was told, in no uncertain terms, that, if a repetition occurred, I would probably find myself jostled and derided for the remainder of the game, but, the damage had been done. By now, I think that everybody around us knew that I was a Liverpool supporter, so the remainder of the match was watched in complete silence. I think that we won!

David Paul

The Psychology of '65

At the end of full time in the '65 FA Cup Final against Leeds, both teams just slumped to the floor, they were tired and needed to rest their legs, anticipating the next thirty minutes of extra time. Upon seeing this, Shankly stormed onto the pitch – I don't believe Shankly ever walked onto a pitch! He said to our players, 'Get on your feet, get on your feet, you've got them beat – just look at them.' It's said that some of the Leeds players just looked at our players standing there, and they were physically, mentally and emotionally beat – it was just too much for some of them.

Gerry Tyrell

The Derby of all Derby Games

It's interesting to reflect that, during the time that we were in the Second Division, Everton didn't win one trophy. We did however play them at Goodison Park in one of

Above: Some of the fans that turned up to witness the triumphant home-coming of Liverpool's Cup-winning team of 1974.

Right: A cherished ticket from the FA Cup Final of 1965, when Liverpool gained a famous 2-1 victory over Leeds United.

EMPIRE STADIUM · WEMBLEY

The Football Association
CUP COMPETITION

Final Tie

Saturday, May 1, 1965, kick off 3 p.m.

YOU ARE ADVISED TO TAKE UP YOUR POSITION BY 2.30 P.M.

CHAIRMAN:
WEMBLEY STADIUM LTD

WEST ENCLOSURE   7/6

ENTER | ENTRANCE
G | 64   STANDING
TURNSTILE

TO BE RETAINED   (See Plan & Conditions on back)

the greatest cup ties that I can ever remember. To me, it was the derby game of all derby games and sticks out in my mind even today. We were actually three from the bottom in the Second Division and they were next to top in the First. That was in 1955 and we beat them 4-0, with Evans scoring two, Liddell getting one, and Acourt getting the other. The ironic thing was, it was Liverpool's first away win during that season, and it was played on 29 January 1955! At the time, one of the records in the hit parade was a song called 'The Happy Wanderer'. A week later, when we played Fulham the crowd began to sing, 'We love to go a-wandering across the park to play, and when we go a-wandering we win our first away'. Fortunately, we won that away game too – the final result being 2-1.

Gerry Tyrrell

The Leicester Semi-Final of '63

One of the biggest disappointments for any fan of Liverpool must be the Leicester Semi-final of 1963. Myself and two friends had queued in the car park at Anfield overnight to make sure that we got tickets for the game.

About ten o'clock at night we walked along to the ground – one friend lived in Grasmere Street and the other lived in St Ambrose Grove, which is further down Breck Road. Kenny's mother made us a whole load of sandwiches enough to sink a ship you would think. We had flasks of tea and flasks of water and overcoats on. As it happens, the Semi-final wasn't due to be played until the end of March. The weather was bloody

There are very few teams in Europe that will ever be able to boast silverware like ours.

freezing. We queued for ages and, at about half-past two or so in the morning, we'd finished the sandwiches, we'd finished the coffee and tea and Kenny said, 'Give me the stuff, I'll go back home, get my mother to give us some refills and then I'll come back.' So that left two of us there and we waited and we waited and we waited, but Kenny never came back. At ten o'clock in the morning there was a huge queue of people, all waiting for tickets. We knew that we'd be okay, as we were in the first hundred or so. Eventually, I got my ticket and Alf got his ticket. By this time the two of us were frozen, hungry and thirsty! So we thought that we'd walk back down and find out where Kenny had got to – what's Foxy done? We hadn't got out of the car park and there he was alongside us with his ticket in his hand. What had happened was that he'd gone out of the gates to go home and when he came back the police wouldn't let him in. So he had the tea and the sandwiches and the coffee to himself, but he never came back till half-past seven in the morning. Effectively, we'd waited for nothing, because we too could have come up with him at half-past seven. As soon as we got the tickets it was straight down to Crown Coaches in St John's Lane where we booked the tickets. We were all looking forward to what Liverpool were going to do to Leicester. The match was due to be played at Hillsborough in Sheffield, so we set off quite early. When we got up on the top of Woodhead Pass, the coach burst into flames. Everybody got off the coach, and we were all standing on this bloody stupid road, where two steps back and we'd fall about three hundred feet, and two steps forward, and we'd be run over by one of the continuous convoy of HGVs. The coach was on fire, there were no mobile phones then and a guy in a flat-backed lorry stopped. There were fifty people on this coach, so all of us climbed onto the back of this flat-back. Everybody had their arms

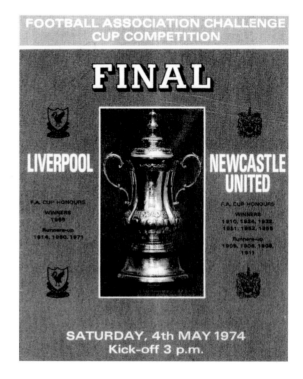

The official programme for the FA Cup Final of 1974. Liverpool had a convincing 3-0 win against Newcastle United.

around everybody else, it was the only way we could stay on. Conversely, if one went, then we all went! Anyway, we got into Sheffield, and as we approached Hillsborough – we all had tickets for Leppings Lane we found that the gates had been locked, and they wouldn't let us in! We'd all got tickets, and we were all banging away, there were one or two choice words used, but the gates stayed shut. They opened the gates for us at half-time, so we got ourselves a place and found out that Leicester were winning 1-0 and, if my memory serves me right, Mike Stringfellow had scored the goal. Anyway, it was 1-0 when we got in and the game finished 1-0, even though we watched Liverpool batter them for the second forty-five minutes. Leicester only crossed the half-way line about three times in the second half. The catalogue of events was that we'd queued all night; we'd been in a coach that had burst into flames; we got a lift on a flat-backed lorry; we couldn't get into the ground and, when we got in, we were getting beat 1-0. Leicester went to the Cup Final and Liverpool didn't – keep it!

Alan Reason

It was after Five in the Morning when Dad Arrived Home

On 20 February 1962 we had a replay against Preston North End. It was the Fifth Round of the Cup, and we'd only managed a draw earlier in the week. Dad was determined to go, even though it was bitterly cold, and there was snow on the ground. We could only manage to draw again. We knew that Dad would be late home because of the extra time, but when it got past midnight, mum was beginning to get very worried. The train was never very early in bad weather. As a young lad I was allowed to wait up with mum. Two o'clock came and dad still hadn't arrived home. By this time we were both dropping off to sleep. When it got to four o'clock Mum was beginning to fear the worst. Well, just after five o'clock in the morning Dad got home, freezing and very, very tired.

Joe Sullivan

She Didn't Want the Knickers

We were playing against Newcastle in the Cup Final. The date was 4 May 1974. I remember it well, as my wife was due to give birth to our first child. I was a little torn as to whether or not I should go to the match, but the decision was not as difficult as I thought it might be! We had a great day. I remember going into Soho and having my hair dyed – everyone seemed to have fancy hair-dos that day, even the Newcastle supporters. I then made a serious error of judgement: I bought my wife a little present from London – the smallest pair of knickers you've ever seen. We hired a car, so that we could get back to Liverpool a bit quicker. When I went to the hospital, she was so upset when I gave her my little present. She still had a figure like the side of a house. I don't think that she got over that. Sharon was born the day after.

Ronnie Bracegirdle

The girls from the
Bullring.

Mum Thought that it was a Darts Match

On the Friday evening, my dear Dad told my Mum that he was off to a darts match
with some of his mates from the local pub. He didn't arrive home that night. He still
wasn't home on the Saturday. Eventually, late on Sunday afternoon, he did come home.
He'd been down to Wembley to watch the Cup Final against Arsenal – unfortunately,
we lost 2-0.

David Boyes

The Secret Hiding Place

When we went to Wembley, which was almost every year, for a final of one kind or
another, we three girls had a very special place to hide our tickets so that they wouldn't
get pinched. And, of course, people were always asking for spares or swops, so that
they could be together with their mates and a couple of times we too would have to
get swops so that we could be together and when we did, whoever we were swopping
with, their eyes would nearly pop out, because we had to get our tickets out of the
special secret hiding place. Up would come the leg of the jeans, down would come the
zip on the leg of the boots, and there would be the ticket at the bottom of the boots
– people really did wonder what was happening!

Marilyn Clay

The Blackest Day

The day couldn't have started better. We'd travelled to our cottage in Yorkshire the night before and enjoyed a very pleasant evening. Then, on the Saturday morning itself, we'd woken up to bright skies, ready to enjoy the whole of the day as it unfolded. After a very gentle morning, as we sorted out our itinerary for the day, we made our way down to the Wagon and Horses, a friendly hostelry in Oxspring, some two miles away. We enjoyed a superb pub lunch, and then got into the car for the short journey to Sheffield. As we drove out of the car park, with the good wishes of the manager and some of the regulars, we broke into quite spontaneous song. The strains of *Here we go, here we go, here we go* filled the car until we got caught up in some of the very heavy traffic making its way to Hillsborough. We weren't worried, as we'd allowed plenty of time for the game. Also, we wanted to experience the build-up to what was billed as being one of the matches of the season – the FA Cup Semi-final between Liverpool and Nottingham Forest – two of the most experienced cup teams in the whole of the Football League.

Directly after leaving the car, we were denied easy access to the ground, as all of the side streets around the stadium had, for some unaccountable reason, been blocked off. Instead, we joined the mounting number of people, albeit jubilant ones, being herded and funnelled into the turnstiles at the Leppings Lane end of the stadium. Even at this early stage, it was obvious that something was awry, or at least not quite right. There appeared to be an unusually heavy surge at the turnstiles and very few police in attendance. In the melee, I was separated from my father-in-law, a fellow supporter who accompanied me to all Liverpool matches, both of us having been season ticket holders for over twenty years. When we eventually did get into the ground, the time was fast approaching ten to three. I felt a bit the 'worse for wear', having taken some crushing at the turnstiles, but my father-in-law, who was approaching seventy, had bruised ribs and was feeling distinctly off-colour. The next memory that's uppermost in my mind is seeing a line of some twenty to thirty policemen inside the ground, apparently doing nothing whatsoever, and just waiting for instructions from a more senior officer. I suggested, not in the politest of English, that they would be better deployed on the outside of the ground. My statement was received with some disdain. Making our way to the seats, we were just in time to see the players come out onto the field. However, by now, more of the collective attention was being focussed on the quite clearly overcrowded terrace at the Leppings Lane end of the field. An older gentleman, who was sat on my left, commented with obvious feeling, that his son was somewhere on that terrace. By now, most people around us were beginning to question just what was happening in the far terrace, and were beginning to suggest that, if nothing was done to alleviate the situation, somebody would be injured and possibly killed. Mayhem then broke out, with people climbing from the upper terrace, and dropping down to the lower terrace – a very precarious move. By now, a line of police had assembled in front of the ground, in an effort to stop the crowd, as they apparently thought that they were going to run onto the pitch. As we now know, the truth was very different from this. It wasn't the fans wanting to run onto the pitch, it was simply that they had nowhere else to go.

Although the game itself had started a few minutes previously, not many people were paying too much attention to what was happening on the field of play, the attention of the crowd was now very firmly fixed on the Leppings Lane end. As the crowd came spilling out, the police were still doing their utmost to contain them – still obviously of the collective opinion that the fans just wanted to invade to pitch. Before too long, even they realised that something was very seriously wrong now. The next tragic action was for some fans to rip advertising hoardings off their mountings, and use them as impromptu stretchers. Initially, there was a trickle, just one or two people being carried across the field, play having long since ceased at six minutes past three. Gradually, more and more fans came to help, and then, the first one with a jacket completely covering the body. Turning to my father-in-law, I said 'This can only mean one thing'. As the gruesome afternoon extended, more stretchers were coming across, with clothing completely covering those being carried. It was clear that, even at that time, the police weren't quite sure what was going on. In fact, it wouldn't be an exaggeration to suggest that they really hadn't got a clue! Even now, the scenes that followed are still too vivid in my memory to recount. All I can say is that we were lucky and eventually did get back home to the cottage, deeply distressed. That evening the phone didn't stop ringing. We had phone calls from Germany, Kuala Lumpur and lots of friends and family from around the country who knew that I'd have been at that particular game. For all the wrong reasons, a day which I can never forget.

David Paul

Sleeping Through the Final

My favourite Liverpool memories, despite the successful trophy-winning years of my childhood, come from more recent barren seasons. Typically, they surround the actions of both myself and also my friends and the situations that have arisen when we have followed our glorious team across the land.

Our journey to the 1996 FA Cup Final, wearing red and green 'Scouse' wigs, began with a drinking contest between myself, Ian and 'star of the day' John. It started at 7 a.m. at Ian's house and continued via the motorway network whilst en route to London. During this time our designated driver, Steve, could only sulk at our enjoyment. Arriving at Wembley by 11 a.m. we decided to continue our 'sesh' at the nearest pub.

When we arrived the pub was full to the brim with United fans. Rather than be discouraged by this, we entered the pub and began to sing the praises of our favourite team. Many people believed that there would be nothing but trouble at this Cup Final, because of the well documented rivalry between the clubs, but from my own experience nothing could be further from the truth. The lead up to the game was all spent in good humour, with the Liverpool fans triumphing in the singing war. After all how can any team compete with the history of Liverpool FC! With just fifteen minutes to go before kick-off, the four of us left the pub, in what can only be described as poor condition. As three of us made for the stadium, Ian decided to give way to his superstitious nature and made for the nearest policewoman to ask for a good luck kiss. After two to three minutes of protest from the girl in blue, and two to three minutes of the rest of us being convinced that Ian was going to be arrested, she gave in and let the drunken red and green-haired freak peck her on the cheek.

After entering the stadium, John's day took a marked turn for the worse. After completing the mass chorus of You'll Never Walk Alone, John decided it was time to fall asleep – only to wake up just in time for the final whistle. Some might say that he probably had a better afternoon's entertainment than the rest of us, but try telling that to him!

Mark Howard

The First Liverpool v Everton Cup Final

When it was the first Cup Final between Liverpool and Everton, we ran a coach from our house. That really was very exciting. Everyone on the coach, both Reds and Blues, were very friendly towards one another. The atmosphere on the coach as they left was warm and friendly, and it was just the same when they returned home early on Sunday morning. Some people on the coach were dressed from head to toe in red and white and others were similarly dressed, but in blue and white. They all met at our house first and had a good solid breakfast together before setting off for Wembley. I didn't go to the game, I did all the food preparation, both for the breakfast itself and for the loads of food and drink which was packed onto the coach before they set off. Our local priest was on board, as were some ex-Liverpool players.

Angela Parry

Standing ticket for the first Merseyside Cup Final, 10 May 1986. Liverpool won 3-1.

Liverpool playing against Swansea in the Third Round of the FA Cup in the 1935/1936 season. Liverpool won this game 1-0 at home, scoring with a free kick followed by a header from Wright. They lost 2-0 in the next round, also at home, to Arsenal. The Liverpool team during that campaign included: Bradshaw; Carr; Cooper; Dabbs; Howe; Johnson; McDougall; Niewenhuys; Riley; Savage and Wright.

The Merseyside Cup Final

When Liverpool played Everton in that first memorable Cup Final it was a sight worth seeing. One half of our coach was blue and white, and the other half was red and white. On the way we had to pick up the priest, Father Brian Crane, at St Mary's – he was an Evertonian. He came out of church after saying mass. He had a blue and white hat on, a blue and white umbrella and a blue and white scarf. At the time he was still dressed in his clerical garb. You'd never see anything like it anywhere in the country – two sets of opposing supporters sharing the same coach. Opposing fans also went down in cars together that day. They went by train, and some flew down. But wherever and however they were travelling, they were all together. It really was a Merseyside final.

Paul Parry

Taking the Coach to Wembley

The first ever Merseyside FA Cup Final was due to be played at Wembley on 10 May 1986. We'd travelled to one or two of the earlier rounds of the Cup, but going to Wembley was quite a different matter. To begin with, it was down in London, and the travelling costs alone would be fairly horrendous. Secondly, and more importantly, the cost of the Cup Final tickets was very expensive. Although being season ticket holders more or less guaranteed us a ticket, there was never any indication as to the cost of the ticket. When the ticket information was eventually released, we had been allocated medium price tickets. The decision therefore was whether or not the cost of the day out in London, and the pleasure which it may give, exceeded the pleasure we would derive from buying a few beers to drink at home, and watching the match from the comfort of our own armchairs. The first option won hands down!

I went down to Anfield and queued for hours in the pouring rain. The mood of the people in the queue seemed to suggest that, even though it was raining today, when it came to the final itself, we would all be smiling, because we were going to beat Everton – the second Premier League side on Merseyside!

The great day came. We'd opted to travel down by coach, as the added cost of the rail tickets made the overall costs for the day quite prohibitive. At six o'clock in the morning, a motley, but alert, group of football fans were stood at the Victoria monument in Widnes waiting for the coach to transport us to Wembley. Judging from the conversation in the group, most people considered that six o'clock in the morning was far too early to be setting off for a game which wasn't scheduled to start until three o'clock in the afternoon. When the coach did eventually arrive, most of us realised just why we'd been asked to assemble at such an ungodly hour. It looked as though it was an old coach which had, many years ago been used for the schools run, but had subsequently been pensioned off some considerable time ago. Also, if the early speed on the motorway was any indication of our journey time, then it was quite obvious that we would need all of the nine hours, and maybe more, to get to Wembley in time for the kick-off.

There was some initial degree of tension between the fans, as Liverpool supporters were juxtaposed with Everton supporters. However, when one or two beers had been

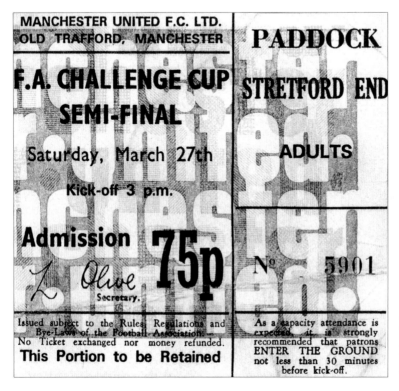

Match ticket for the Semi-final against Everton. Liverpool won 2-1.

quaffed and the odd one exchanged, the atmosphere lightened somewhat, and we all settled down for a pleasant morning's drinking and talking. Some little time later the inevitable happened. Half of the people on the coach needed to pull into the services for the obvious reason, but the coach driver was adamant that he had a schedule to maintain, and he must get to the outskirts of London by one o'clock at the very latest. By this time, we'd gone past the first available services, and we weren't due to get to the next one for some thirty miles – at least another half hour in this old banger. Temperatures were beginning to rise in direct proportion to the pressure on respective bladders. Fortunately, the driver relented, and thirty-five minutes later there was a mass exodus as fifty-five supporters, sporting scarves and banners, were rapidly disgorged from the coach. Whilst not wishing to go into unnecessary detail, suffice it to say that there was considerable pressure on the limited facilities available!

Ten minutes later, and in a much better collective mood, we were on the coach again and heading towards the capital. By now we were all singing and the journey time didn't seem to be as important as it had earlier in the day. The laughter was rocking the coach as we saw for the first time the famous twin towers of Wembley. Unfortunately, because of the several unscheduled stops which we'd had to make whilst travelling down the motorway, we weren't able to get into the Wembley coach park. In fact, the coach in front of us got the very last place! Needless to say, this didn't please our driver too much. He suggested that, after the game, we should aim to be somewhere in this particular vicinity, and he would endeavour to find us – no doubt thinking about the tip which he was hoping to get at the end of the day.

Liverpool going out of the 1968 FA Cup.

It was an exciting game and, of course, we got the result that we wanted. Quite justifiably, Liverpool won 3-1. Obviously, we waited until our victorious team mounted those famous steps to take the FA Cup. The victory was that much sweeter, knowing that we were taking the Cup from the hands of the vanquished Everton team. Next we had to find the coach! By the time everything was sorted, it was moving on to six o'clock, and to say that the streets around Wembley were crowded would be a gross understatement. There was traffic on both sides of us, as well as being in front and behind us. We were totally hemmed in. It was like this all the way out of London, until we eventually hit the motorway some two hours later. Needless to say, by this time, most of the passengers, half of whom were ecstatic because their team had won, and the other half of whom were drowning their sorrows because their team had lost, irrespective of which side you had been supporting, wanted to stop for the loo! However, the driver had other ideas. His main concern was to drop us off in Liverpool, and to get his coach back to the garage. Our speed up the motorway didn't appear to be very much quicker than it had been on the outskirts of London, as there really was very heavy traffic. Somebody spotted a sign which indicated that there was a services in ten miles. By this time we were all absolutely desperate for a loo, and the coach driver – on pain of death – agreed to pull in. It didn't work out like this. When we got to the services some fifteen minutes later, there was a queue of traffic including a line of several coaches waiting to go into the service area. By this time, the police were forbidding any other traffic to stop, so, reluctantly, we had to carry on to the

A ticket from the FA Cup Final of 1977 when, unfortunately, Liverpool lost 2-1 to Manchester United.

next service station some thirty miles further up the motorway. How people contained themselves – and maybe some didn't – I shall never know. It was now getting late in the evening, and although the driver was trying to make as much time as he could, there was a regulator fitted to the coach, which limited our speed to sixty miles per hour, but, in practice, I'm sure that it had been regulated nearer to fifty! We didn't arrive back in Liverpool until well after two o'clock in the morning, so by the time that we made our way home from the bus station, it was almost three o'clock when we were getting to bed. I vowed that night never to go to Wembley again by coach – and I never have!

David Paul

Phil Taylor's Rag Doll

In 1950 we were runners-up to Arsenal in the FA Cup Final. On the way home from Wembley, somebody threw a rag doll to Phil Taylor and, for years after that, Evertonians would gleefully say that all we brought home from Wembley was a rag doll – in fact I think it's still at Anfield. The strange thing was that we'd beaten Arsenal in both League games that year. This made us one of the strongest favourites ever to win the Cup. The other occasion when we were red-hot favourites was when we played Wimbledon in the FA Cup Final. Ironically, despite being favourites, we lost both games.

Gerry Tyrrell

Kenny Dalglish runs rampant against Exeter City in a cup-tie at Anfield.

Geoff Strong's Influence

We then had the St John and Yeats years and we won the Cup for the first time, if you remember, and the liver birds were still on the Liver Building. We brought in a player from Arsenal, Geoff Strong. In my view, Geoff Strong was more influential in the Cup Final than really could have been imagined at the time, because he kept the pace down. Once Liverpool had scored against Leeds, Geoff Strong in actual fact came into his own and dictated the play – he slowed the game up to suit Liverpool's passing game. Remember, our game had been built on the passing game. We passed the ball, passed the ball, passed the ball, until such time when one of our forwards had run into such a position that the ball could be released to him. We still play the same game today. Unfortunately, the way we've been performing just recently, it's not as successful as what it used to be.

Harold S. Scott

Going to Wembley with My Sisters

On 29 April 1950, we went down to Wembley to watch Liverpool play Arsenal in the Cup Final. It was teaming down with rain, we'd had an awful journey down, having first to get the train to Manchester and then transfer to another to take us on to London and then we had to make our way to Wembley. To cap the lot we lost, but we still enjoyed our day out.

June Titherington

A wet but jubilant end to our long journey to Wembley – 29 April 1950 – when Liverpool lost 2-0 to Arsenal.

Just Look at the Idiot on that Coach

On another occasion we went to see Liverpool play Aston Villa in the Semi-final of the Cup. It was a great match with Peter Thompson doing his usual dribbling with his head down and not knowing where anybody was. Also it was a nice score again, I think that we won that one 2-1. On the day I wore a cardboard head-dress which I dyed red. Everything was fine until the rain came down. It was raining particularly hard when we were looking for our coach after the match. Unbeknown to everyone on the coach, they'd actually moved it during the game, but hadn't bothered to tell us. We eventually found it, after a twenty-minute search. By this time all the dye had come out of the cardboard and had been soaked into my clothes and I was streaked both muddy and red. Added to this, because the coaches were now full, the only coach that I could get on was not with my mates.

Whilst all this was happening, the Grand National was being run over at Aintree. I'd managed to place a bet before leaving Liverpool. As the coach which I should have been on was overtaking us on the motorway, one of my mates – a very funny guy – was making signs to me, which I took to mean 'How did you go on in the Grand National?' I showed the thumbs up to him, signalling 'Fantastic!' In fact, with the whole of their bus roaring with laughter, a running commentary was being given – something on the lines of, 'You're a pillock aren't you? There you are, you're all in red, what an idiot, coming out here like this, getting totally soaked. And look, there's the red hat, and there he is. Look you can see how thick he is gentlemen, he's got his thumb up, and he's signalling to me'. It was only by sheer coincidence, some two years later, that I found out that my mate was actually taking the mickey out of me. Somebody who happened to be on the coach that day remembered the dishevelled individual on the other coach, and recognised him as being me!

Trevor Burke

I've Found the Tickets

One away cup-tie Saturday, two precious tickets couldn't be found. I don't think that Martin's friend could believe it, but, undaunted, they left. I made one more careful search, but we'd already had the house upside-down. Searching through a heap of old newspapers, I found the envelope with its precious contents. I dashed upstairs, dragged one of our student lodgers out of bed and, stopping only to pull on a pair of trousers and a jumper over my nightie and slippers, I got the car out and went hurtling off to Lime Street Station. John leapt out while I drove round the block a few times. He found Martin and Tony still queuing for the train. What a close shave and what a tremendous relief!

Jo Farrell

My Dad the Unknown Hero

The first time that we played against Everton in the Cup Final, the game we won 3 - 1, I went down with my dad and a friend of ours, Gordon. There were a lot of forged tickets on sale that year and the crowds were absolutely incredible. We were crushed all the time

We've got the Cup – again!

that we were waiting to go into the stadium. People who had forged tickets were being turned away by the police, but not until their tickets had been checked at the top of the stairs. What was happening then, was that whilst some people were still trying to get in, others were trying to make their way out. It was chaos. There was an old chap in front of us who just lost his footing. He was in grave danger of being trampled. Being six foot four, my dad was able to hold back some of the crowd until we could drag him out.

Ambulance men were very quickly on the scene, and he was rushed off to hospital – the story about the unknown hero of Wembley made the national news later that evening. In the meantime, the queues had really got bad, as it was now just before three o'clock. Gordon, me and my dad just couldn't get in. The police did let us in when we explained what had happened, but we still couldn't get up to our seats. We ended up watching the game on a television screen under the main stand. Two hundred miles just to watch the game on telly!

Sharon Bracegirdle

We Got There in a Cattle Truck

We were playing a Charity Shield game against Man U – it was in the days before the event was staged at Wembley. This particular game was at Old Trafford. We got one of the special trains which took us from Lime Street Station into the centre of Manchester. We then had to change and get a train out to the ground itself. Well, as we were herded into this train, and that's the correct expression to use, we found to our great dismay, that we were actually being loaded into cattle trucks. Yes, the real live things – trucks used to transport cattle. We couldn't believe it then and I've never forgotten it since!

Don Smith

No doubt about it – Liverpool are out of the 1968 FA Cup.

Cup Dilemma

We'd taken the Football Special to see one of our many games played against Scunthorpe. It was a particularly important game and it only cost twenty-seven bob on the Football Special. The unfortunate thing was, Liverpool were due to play against Oldham the following Saturday in a Cup match and we also wanted to go to that game. However, the tickets were being sold at the reserves game that day and it looked as though we wouldn't be able to get one. When we arrived at Scunthorpe station, we were met by two Liverpool directors, one a chap called Richards and I can't remember the other fellow's name. They'd decided that it was unfair on the fans who were travelling to see the Scunthorpe game, knowing that they wouldn't be able to buy tickets for next Saturday's game. They decided to take a load of tickets to Scunthorpe to make sure that we didn't get left out. I thought that that was a tremendous gesture – a great attitude – and they sold us the tickets there and then. That was the way the club was run then; the club was on its way up.

Gerry Tyrrell

Dad's Mate Got My Ticket

The 1971 FA Cup Final was to be my first ever. I couldn't begin to describe the anticipation I was experiencing at the thought of going down to London to watch my team play. I went to school on the Friday morning, but I wasn't concentrating on the lessons. When I got home, Mum had packed my bag all ready for the following day. My dad went to the pub that night, as was his practice on a Friday evening. He'd gone to his local – the Sea Dog. But, instead of coming home later that night, he went straight down to Wembley.

Match ticket for the 1971 FA Cup Final.

My ticket, which he happened to have in his pocket, was given to one of his mates. He didn't get home till Monday afternoon, and Mum really gave him 'down the banks'.

Paul Stewart

Another Armani Suit Ruined

Liverpool were playing Fulham in one of the cup competitions down in London. I'd been to a business meeting, supposedly the chief executive of a public company – but could I get a ticket, could I heck! All my contacts had failed me, but not my indomitable feelings of support for Liverpool. I decided that I'd go around the local pubs in the hope of buying a ticket. I was like a sixteen-year-old again walking around these pubs, with some very doubtful looking Fulham fans also in the market for tickets. They were offering all sorts of ridiculous prices. By now the rain was coming down – four people were killed in the London area that night as a result of the weather. There was thunder and lightening – the whole thing. I was wearing perhaps my most expensive ever suit, carrying a borrowed umbrella and getting absolutely soaked as the wind and the rain were blown into my face. The suit was quite clearly ruined. Two touts approached me out of the mist saying that they'd heard that I was looking for a ticket. I said that I really needed the covered area and they sold me a ticket for what they assured me was the covered end when actually it was the opposite, it was open to the elements – obviously the touts around London are not as honest as the touts around Liverpool, because they're always honest as everyone knows! So, when I got into the ground after being two hours in the rain, I actually put my umbrella up, only to be greeted by thirty or forty rather large Scousers behind me, who told me that they'd put the umbrella in a certain indelicate place if I didn't put it down. So, I put the umbrella down. We won, we didn't play very well and, at six o'clock the following morning, I found myself in hospital with the shakes and violently throwing up – another story of dedication to Liverpool Football Club!

Even now, at forty-nine, there's something that strikes me every time that I go to a Liverpool match and that's the fact that I still have the same passion, the same lunatic enthusiasm, the same rush of adrenalin, whether we win or lose. And, when we do lose, which is slightly more frequently than it used to be, I'm still bad tempered and really depressed till probably Tuesday evening. I don't know whether it ever gets to other people that way, but that certainly is me!

Trevor Burke

Three Feet of Snow

Early on in the '62/63 season, we were due to play Wrexham away in the Cup. I hitched a lift through the tunnel. When I got out of the car on the Birkenhead side, there was a number of people thumbing lifts. Eventually a guy in a box van stopped, and we all piled into the back, just like carcasses hanging up on hooks. Anyway, he took us all the way to Wrexham. There had been heavy snow during the week and there was some considerable doubt as to whether or not the game would be played. The ground staff at Wrexham were quite resourceful however, what they'd done is that they'd cleared the pitch of all the snow by throwing the snow over the wall – they used to have these three foot walls all around the ground at that time – and all they'd done was to throw the snow over, and let it pile up on the spectators' side. We stood there with snow past our knees to watch that game. Anyway, we won that particular game 3-1 but that season's competition finished with being beaten by Leicester.

Alan Reason

We won the Cup! Crowds of jubilant fans in 1974.

CHAPTER 4

LIVERPOOL PLAYERS

I Still Can't Understand Why He Got Rid of Alonso

Benitez will be judged against many illustrious Liverpool managers. His style will certainly be compared with many of the more recent managers, as will his man-management. He always appeared to be totally aloof, and I've heard tell that there have been one or two heated discussions in the dressing room and at the training ground. But, it's all over now, and I'm one of the many supporters who won't be sad to see the back of him. The only good thing that he did, as far as I'm concerned, was to bring Torres to Liverpool, but I don't know whether he'll stay now, especially if he has a good run in the World Cup. I still can't understand why he got rid of another one of our better players, Alonso. I know that they had their disagreements, but Alonso had an incredible understanding of the game, and was an excellent player. Everyone around me has regretted him leaving, and Liverpool have certainly felt like a different team since he left, and not a better team!

Sam Weston

Billy Liddell – A Man Amongst Men

Players these days are coming to their form much younger than they did in the period that we're actually talking about just after the war. Perhaps it's because they always appeared to be mature people, you know, and had the stability of a wife and family and things like that, which you don't necessarily have today. But then we came into the Billy Liddell period. There weren't the massive transfer fees at that time and Billy Liddell, make no bones about it, was a man amongst men, both as a person – he was a quality person in his life and has remained so all of his life – but also as a footballer. I can think back to goals that Liddell scored and it would have been impossible for players these days to score, considering the type of ball that they were using at that time, which you know were the heavy leather balls, not the artificial material that they're using today. They used to collect water and they would be extremely heavy, but Liddell used to be able to propel down the wing so fast – he was a Scottish international – and could he take a free kick! I've seen Liddell score many times directly from a corner to save the game for Liverpool. At one time they called it Liddellpool – but that's unfair to the man, because he was a man of great stature, a man of worth. I don't think that I ever

Above: Alun Evans – Liverpool's first £100,000 signing. Seen here with Eddie Sullivan.

Right: Kevin Keegan sitting in the players' lounge with Jamie Dowd.

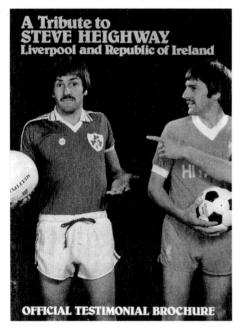

A Tribute to STEVE HEIGHWAY
Liverpool and Republic of Ireland

OFFICIAL TESTIMONIAL BROCHURE

CHAIRMAN OF THE COMMITTEE

A man who has done himself and Soccer proud

JEFF TINNION says . . .

STEVE HEIGHWAY is a first-class footballer and first-class as a person. That's recommendation enough for me to add that I feel privileged to be the chairman of his testimonial committee, and I know that the members of the committee have worked hard – and willingly – on Steve's behalf, not least because of the high regard they have for him.

As it happened, I first came into contact with Steve through his team-mate, Ray Clemence, and in our business dealings I quickly learned one thing: Steve is reliable, and he never lets you down. The same can be said of him whenever he has worn the red jersey of Liverpool or the green of the Republic of Ireland. Apart from skill, he has always been a 100 per-center.

A lot of work has gone into the job of making Steve's testimonial season a success, and it says much for the man himself that so many people have been ready to co-operate and contribute in different ways. Which is my cue to thank sponsors, advertisers and supporters for their generous response in ensuring that things have gone smoothly.

Having said my piece, I'll just add that many, many people will echo the sentiments expressed by the famous names who have contributed to this brochure . . . over the past 10 years Steve Heighway has done himself and football – at club and international level – proud. And, in the process, he has given pleasure to the game's fans.

Left and below: The front cover of the programme for Steve Heighway's Testimonial. Jeff Tinnion knew Steve Heighway very well – he was the chairman of the Testimonial Committee.

saw Liddell get his name taken, or even foul against other players. Truly, he was a superb sportsman.

Harold S. Scott

'Sammy' and the Market Stall

Because of working on the markets, we mainly used to go to mid-week games because we always worked at weekends. When we worked with Joe we'd try to get to the match. Terry and Joe, whose mum was about sixty and sold ladies' clothes on the market, used to be right opposite to us. We were all mates and we'd say, 'Are you going to the match?' This depended upon whether or not their mother gave them the time off – at the time these guys were pushing forty. Their best mate was Sammy Lee and they used to come to the market in 'Greaty' [Great Homer Street Market] with a pram, and their stall was loaded on top of the pram. They'd come from the flats at the back and walk down to the market.

After this pattern had been established for some time, Sammy Lee started going down with them and everybody would joke with him, 'Are you getting a game today Sammy?' – this was about six o'clock in the morning in 'Greaty'. He'd come down, near enough every other Saturday with the lads – the two brothers who were his mates. It was amazing, even at the time when he played the odd game for Liverpool, just before he became really famous, he'd still be there on 'Greaty', helping to put the stall up. All the Evertonians would have a go at him, then we'd have a go at him and all he was doing was helping to put up a little ten-foot stall for the brothers' mother. After the stall had been erected, they'd go back and bring all the clothes which they were

Liverpool Football Club – English League Champions, 1963/1964.

PLAYERS' TRAINING RULES

AND INSTRUCTIONS.

———

1.—All players shall attend at the Ground for training at 10 a.m. daily (Match days excepted) and shall be under the orders of the Trainers for the rest of the day. Players must not leave the ground before 12-30 p.m.

2. At the commencement of each season, every player must undergo a Medical examination and carry out the instructions prescribed by the Medical Officer of the Club. In cases of illness or accident, players must notify the Trainer or Manager, or arrange that he is notified immediately. Medical Officer of the Club — Dr. Reid, 111, Priory Road, Anfield, Liverpool, 4 (Telephone : Anfield 724). Doctor's hours: Morning, 9-10.30; Evening, 6-8.

3.—Players must not bring friends into the Dressing Room or Billiard Room without permission.

4.—Smoking in the Dressing Room during training hours is strictly forbidden.

5.—On match days all players must be at the ground 45 minutes before the advertised time of kick-off and at the station 15 minutes before the train starts.

6.—Players are entirely responsible for ascertaining the particulars on the Team Notices which are fixed in the Dressing Room each week.

7.—All players not selected to play in any team must be at the ground on match days and report to the Trainer in time to strip and play should any emergency arise. Players not taking part in Saturday matches must report at 10 a.m. on the following Monday for training.

Above and below: The Players' Training Rules and Instructions, as given to Ken Whitfield for the 1952/1953 season.

8.—During the playing season players desiring to go Home at Week-ends must obtain the consent of the Manager.

9.—Players shall do everything necessary to get and keep themselves in the best possible condition during and after training hours so as to render the most efficient service to the Club. No player shall take part in Dancing after Wednesday of each week.

Players must not frequent Clubs where gambling takes place or intoxicants served.

10.—The Club will not be responsible for the paying of Players' wages for any period of incapacity due to accidents while motoring.

11.—No player shall write articles for the press or interview the press without first obtaining permission of the Manager.

12.—When on the field of play all players are under the orders of the Captain of the team, and all instructions from the Directors to the Captain must be conveyed through the Manager or such other person appointed.

13.—Any player wilfully disobeying the orders of any instructions embodied in these rules will be dealt with at the discretion of the Directors.

14.—Players are responsible for the studding of their own boots. The Trainers will attend to them as desired.

D. WELSH,
Manager.

hoping to sell that day. Once everything was sorted out – and mum had given the okay to the two forty-year-olds – they'd sit back and listen to the game on Merseyside. It wasn't very often that they were allowed to go to the game itself!

Mark Rochford

How Many Balls Are There?

I'd gone to Anfield with Alison to pick up some balls to put into the kids' Christmas stockings. We came out of the ground and drove towards Aintree for some other shopping. I happened to see Neil Ruddock's car just in front of us – you can't miss it, as his registration number is HED IT. I thought that it might be a good idea to get the balls autographed, so I followed him to the Retail Park. It ended up that he was parked on one side of a hedge, and I happened to be parked on the other side. I popped my head over and asked if he'd be good enough to sign the balls. He didn't mind at all – but when it got to the fifth one, I think that he'd had enough!

Keith Corcoran

Harrower's Determination

When Liverpool were coming out onto the pitch one day in a match against Scunthorpe, Harrower slipped and fell over. Most of the Scunthorpe players started laughing at him

Jan Molby with some of his fans.

in a derisory manner. He was full of Scottish blood and when he got up he just glared at them and gave the ball a boot down the field. He'd kicked that ball in sheer malice, but that day he gave an inspired performance. I honestly feel that that performance has rarely been bettered by anyone in a Liverpool shirt.

Gerry Tyrrell

Kippax from Burnley

In the mid-forties, we had a brilliant left-winger called Peter Kippax. I saw him play first-team football a number of times – he was a fine player, an inspiration to those around him. The only problem was, Peter would never sign professional papers, he was only ever an amateur player for Liverpool. His father was a millionaire mill-owner from Burnley, so money was just not a consideration as far as he was concerned.

Peter May

St John Sent Off!

The League game against Preston, in the season that we got knocked out of the Cup by them at Anfield, is probably one of the most memorable in my mind. St John was playing and was being marked by the Preston centre half, Tony Singleton. It was a running feud from the moment that the game started. St John was five-eight, five-nine and Singleton was perhaps six-one, six-two. In fact, St John was beating him in the air, primarily because of the ability he had of gaining height for such a small man and Singleton just couldn't cope with him. Eventually, Singleton just smacked St John whilst the referee wasn't looking. St John went down and there was no happy flag-waving linesman. They just let it go! St John suddenly realised that he was on the floor and that the play was all down the other end and he jumped up as if somebody had given him the magic sponge. He ran straight down the pitch to Singleton, never broke his run at all, kicked Singleton right up the arse, turned round and walked off. And all this was without the referee saying a word to him – he just walked off the pitch! He knew that he was going to be sent off, but he laid Singleton on the floor and walked off to a hero's reception. I can still recall the sight of him running towards the Anfield Road end. That one kick, straight up the rear, with Singleton going down like a log. I think that St John made his point!

Alan Reason

A Unique Start at Anfield

St John made his debut for Liverpool in the Liverpool Senior Cup Final at Goodison Park. On the night we lost 4-3, but St John almost pulled off a superb draw. It might have only been the Liverpool Senior Cup, but at the time we were in the Second Division and Everton were in the First Division. What a game St John played! In the end nobody cared about the result, that was irrelevant. Here was this fellow that they'd bought in from Motherwell, a total unknown, and there he goes and puts three goals into the net. Make no mistake, in spite of what anyone may tell you, he was a complete unknown when he came to Liverpool. His last goal was a tap-in. Roger Hunt could have had it, but he just stood to one side and let the young St John score his hat-trick. In those days, there'd be anything up to 50,000 watching the Liverpool Senior Cup, because, being in different divisions, there were no derby games then. So the Liverpool Senior Cup was the only time we were able to show our skills against Everton. Strangely enough Liverpool and Everton were never drawn against one another until later on in the competition. I don't know what the fraud squad would think about that today!

The other notable feature about St John's unique start to his playing career at Anfield was the fact that he was sent off before he'd even played a League game for us. We were playing a friendly over in Czechoslovakia and he was sent off for dissent. So, before he'd actually started his League career for Liverpool, he'd scored three against Everton and been sent off in a friendly – what a start!

Gerry Tyrrell

Signing as a Player

My first husband, who's been dead for many years now, was a good football player. He played many games for different schoolboy sides and then was eventually invited by the manager of Liverpool Football Club, George Kay, to play in a trial match at Melwood. The letter which invited him to the game also informed him which buses would get him to the ground and also told him to bring along his own boots and stockings – very different from what happens today I suspect! As a result of this game he was offered a part-time contract and, for his services, he was paid at the rate of £3 per week. The contract also stated that if he played in the Central League Team, he would receive a further £2 per week. Having said that, the contract did specifically stipulate that: 'The Player hereby agrees to play in an efficient manner and to the best of his ability for the Club'. I wonder if this clause is still included in the current contracts?

Sheila Ramsey

Ray Clemence's Coins

In the seventies, when the great Ray Clemence kept goal for us, opposing fans sometimes used to throw coins at him to distract him and make him lose his concentration. It never worked. There was even a bonus. At the end of the game Ray collected all the coins up, and, making his way over to the young kids who always congregated around his goal, he'd give them these little piles of money. No doubt by this time there was probably quite a few bob in the kitty! Not many goalkeepers would think of making such a kind gesture.

Paul McEvoy

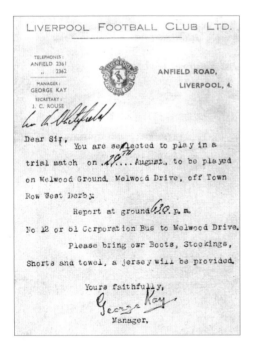

Above left: An invitation to play in a trial match – it's just as well that there was a good bus service!

Above right: Ken gets his contract renewed.

Ray Clemence receiving the *Liverpool Echo* Sports Personality of the Year award.

Above left: McInnes played a couple of seasons for Liverpool in the late 1930s.

Above right: Liverpool had an indifferent start to the 1946/1947 season – winning the first game, losing the second, winning the third and then losing 5-0 to Manchester United. In an effort to strengthen the team, they offered Newcastle United a record fee of £12,500 for Albert Stubbins. The rest you may think is history, but it wasn't quite as easy as that. Everton also liked the looks of Stubbins, and they put in a rival bid. Not being able to decide, Stubbins tossed a coin. Fortunately, it came down in favour of Liverpool! Liverpool went on to win the League that year, assisted by Stubbins' twenty-four goals!

Ron Yeats' Testimonial

I can remember the first time that I took my girlfriend to a match at Anfield. I didn't really want to take her to a League match, as I thought there'd be too many people there and she might get crushed. At the time, the capacity of Anfield was over fifty thousand, I think. Fortunately, Ron Yeats was due to have his testimonial match during the next week and I thought that would be a better game to go to. As we were playing Celtic, I didn't think there would be that many people coming down from Scotland. How wrong can you be? The whole of the Anfield Road end, and quite a lot more of the far end of the stadium, was just festooned in green and white. It was an absolute sell-out, a capacity crowd. We were stood in the Kop, my girlfriend was getting a little crushed, but seemed to be enjoying the game. Then it happened – Yeats scored a goal into the Kop end. The crowd went berserk and Yeats came running over to accept the jubilant acclaim of the Kop. As we were very near to the front, we were actually a little lower than the level of the pitch, Yeats seemed to dominate and fill the entire skyline.

Tim Rutter

Taxi for Harry Smith

The Liverpool forward Alf Arrowsmith had been to the orthopaedic clinic and was now waiting to go home by taxi, which I was ordering.

'Can I have a cab to take Mr Arrowsmith from Broadgreen Outpatients to his home?'
'Right, tell Mr Smith that we'll be round in about ten minutes.'
'NO, not Smith, Mr Arrowsmith.'
'Okay, tell Harry Smith that we'll be there as soon as we can.'
'NO, not Smith, Alfred Arrowsmith.'
'Look, we're very busy here – just tell Harry Smith to be ready at the pickup point.'
End of conversation.

I went back and said to Alf, 'Just for today and to avoid any further confusion, please be Harry Smith.'

Frank McCormack

And Then There Was Fred Morris

One Easter Monday we went to watch Liverpool play at Barnsley. Before the match it was announced over the Tannoy that there were to be some changes in the Liverpool team and instead of Liddell playing at number eleven, Fred Morris would play instead. Now Fred Morris was one of those players who was a 'fringe' player for Liverpool, he'd come from Mansfield and the fans loved him, nonetheless he was an absolutely poor player, but he had a big heart and was a big lad, a big lad, a big Midlands lad. You certainly wouldn't have put Fred Morris in your top hundred Liverpool players, so when the announcement was made a spontaneous cry went up –'Oh no, no Billy!' but Fred came on and scored a hat-trick. Nobody could quite believe it. A few weeks later, however, when we were playing Barnsley at Anfield, Liverpool were awarded a penalty. Fred spotted the ball, but I think that Dunlop in the Everton goal probably had to save it at Goodison – it went that far wide!

Gerry Tyrrell

Liverpool's Classic Half-Backs

I always remember one player that we brought in, he was a fellow named Barry Wilkinson. Now Barry Wilkinson was a player with tremendous potential and, yes, he played in the first team, but in my view he never ever fulfilled that potential as a player. He played for England and this type of thing, but never was he ever one of the great classical half-backs – and Liverpool have a whole series of great classical

A rare shot, featuring three famous Liverpool managers – Bill Shankly, Bob Paisley and Joe Fagan.

half-backs who were influential in the game. Phil Taylor was one of the earliest ones at the end of the war, he played for England, a beautiful, cultured full-back. Then we had the boy who came from Rangers, Shankly brought him from Rangers, beautiful passer of the ball and then, eventually, we got Jan Molby. If you remember, Jan Molby could pass a ball in his sleep, a beautiful player. I've seen Jan Molby pass a ball and produce a goal-scoring situation out of virtually nothing – especially when he passed to that phenomenal player that we had at that time, who was Ian Rush. We had lots of good players at that time, players like Keegan, Toshack and Ian Rush, but their success, in my view, was always built on Liverpool's ability to find that classic half-back from somewhere. It remains, even to this day, to some degree. To my mind I always felt that Jan Molby was one of the finest passers of the ball that I'd ever seen. It was alright for the likes of Keegan to be very spectacular, but Keegan reaped a lot of the benefits of Molby's play. To my mind it was inspiration, Shankly's inspiration, to pair Toshack with Keegan. In fact, I'd go as far as to say that Keegan was never ever the same player after he left Liverpool. I mean he had a lot of success in other clubs, but to my mind he was never ever anything like the player that he'd been as when he was playing alongside Toshack – Toshack was one of the finest players that Liverpool ever had.

Harold S. Scott

Guy Ropes in the Ankle

The Liverpool defender Emlyn Hughes had sustained an ankle injury and, following examination, it was decided that strapping of the joint for a few days would be sufficient. My colleague, carrying out the task explained to Emlyn just what he was going to do. He described the ankle structure as being like guy ropes that stabilise the ankle, some pulling one way, some the other and that by applying strapping in a particular way a synthetic guy rope would be created and this would have a steadying effect. After completing the treatment Emlyn thanked my colleague for his explanation and said that he was surprised to learn that he had guy ropes in his ankles, as he had always believed that he had tendons and ligaments – whoops!

Frank McCormack

Billy's Word's Good Enough

We were on our way down to Worcester. It was snowing some of the time and then raining some of the time and, in those days without the motorways and in those conditions, it took hours to get there. Going down, people were saying, 'The game's going to be called off' and then we'd travel twenty miles further, and we'd think that the game was on again. It was like this all the way down. As I say, it took us ages to get there and when we did arrive, we were cold and wet and miserable, but looking

McInnes, who played for Liverpool in the late 1930s.

forward to our team beating this lowly side. The pitch was worse than a park pitch and this was the Third Round of the FA Cup in 1959! A few hundred loyal supporters had made the difficult journey down and most of us were not very happy at the prospect of a game on this pitch – the feeling was not good! Just then, Billy Liddell came out from the dressing rooms. He told us that if he was asked to play on that pitch then he might well break a leg. The guy in front of me said, 'That'll do for us Billy' and with that everyone dispersed and drove back to Liverpool. Not another word was said. We were down again the following Tuesday, which was the 15 January. I remember it well – we got beat 2-1, with Twentyman scoring our goal. The headlines in the papers the following day said 'Worcester Sauce' – very apt!

David Grooby

St John's Autograph

Many years ago, I took the kids along to a soccer camp and Ian St John happened to be there. Later that evening I was in conversation with him and I asked him for his autograph. Whilst he was signing the autograph, I asked him if he still lived in Maghull. Years before that, when St John lived near to Ron Yeats, a friend of mine also lived in the same area. As kids, we'd gone along to try to get their autographs. I was telling St John how I'd knocked on his door that day. Before I could finish the sentence, he came back, sharp as a razor, and said, 'Yes, and you're still moidering me!'

Keith Corcoran

Jamie Shops in Marks

I went shopping at Marks & Spencer in Warrington. I was with another friend of mine, one of my sons and also one of her children. We saw Jamie Redknapp walking along one of the isles, so we headed up the other way, round the back as it were, so that it wouldn't look as though we were just following him, but rather that we were bumping into him. He came towards us, so we stopped him and got his autograph. He wasn't playing at the time, as he had an ankle injury. I forgot to ask him how it was healing!

Colette Corcoran

Liddell Scored Three

Every derby game that I've ever been to, and that's quite a few, has been exciting, but one game in particular stands out in my mind and that's the one when we played at Goodison in November 1947. I think the gate that day is still the highest-ever recorded at Goodison – a gate of 78,240. It was an exciting game, but what made my day, even more than the 4-1 drubbing which Everton received, was the fact that my idol, the great Billy Liddell scored three of the goals. What a memory!

Peter May

Above left: Wright, transferred from Cowdenbeath in the late 1920s. he played for Liverpool until the early 1930s and was a fine player. Unfortunately, he also scored a few memorable own goals!

Above right: A carton from the early 1930s, suggesting that Wright was the man that they should be passing to.

Gordon Milne's Distribution

The thing about Gordon Milne was his brain was infinitely better than his feet, he was such an intelligent player and could get away from anyone else on the field. He was a fragile player, he tackled like a centurion and his distribution was better than the Post Office! He was an absolutely tremendous player was Gordon Milne.

Gerry Tyrrell

Gerry Byrne

There are probably two or three other games which, for one reason or another, stand out in my memory. One was at Bournemouth when Liverpool played them in an early round of the Cup at Dean Court. During the game Gerry Byrne was carried off with a knee injury that, subsequently, finished his career. It was a totally innocuous tackle and it robbed Liverpool, I thought, of perhaps the best left-back we'd had in maybe twenty-five, or even thirty, years. I thought Byrne was a hell of a player. But, as I say, we went to Dean Court, we got the result that we wanted, but paid a big price for it.

Alan Reason

O. G. White

They then signed the Yeats fellow, and the Yeats lad was a tremendous signing. In those days we also had a centre half called Dick White, and Dick White used to come onto the pitch smoking. For some reason, he insisted on smoking during the kick-in. We bought him from Scunthorpe and he was a very good player. People used to think that his name was 'O. G.', because every week in the programme it said, 'White, OG (own goal)'. In fact, I think that he scored seven own goals during one season. But, as I say, he did the job and was a good player.

Gerry Tyrrell

Peter Thompson

Liverpool were playing Preston in the Cup. They played at Anfield and drew. They then played at Preston and drew after extra time. Then it went to Old Trafford and we were beaten 1-0 by a player called Peter Thompson. He looked a good lad, he looked as though he might have a future in football and, thankfully, he spent that future at Anfield. He didn't score that many goals, but to score the one that knocked us out of the Cup was not amusing – I didn't laugh. But, nonetheless, out of those three games, Liverpool gained Peter Thompson. It's a pity we didn't get Kendall, that would have been nice, but events afterwards proved that we didn't actually need him.

Alan Reason

CHAPTER 5

EUROPEAN GAMES

We Had a 'Whip-Around' for the Pilot

I've been a Liverpool supporter for all of my life. Growing up in Liverpool and soaking up the atmosphere in the ground on match days is something that few other people in this country can imagine. So, when we started to get into Europe, I saved enough money to go on one of the first charter flights out of Speke airport. I worked it so that my shifts were OK at work – I even swapped a night shift with a very understanding Evertonian, but it cost me!

The plane was full as we taxied down the runway and off into Europe. The game was great – we won – and then there was the flight back, straight after the game ended. Everyone was very elated, not only with the result, but also with the fact that we could leave Liverpool in the morning and be back home again less than twenty-four hours later. The flight itself was fairly uneventful, we had a couple of drinks and a few sandwiches that we'd bought at the airport. When the captain said that we'd be touching down at Speke in half an hour, someone suggested that we had a 'whip-around' for the pilot and the crew. The hat was duly passed around, and I think that there was a little unexpected bonus for the crew at the end of that flight. Only Liverpool people could think of anything like that. Can you see that happening these days!

Sam Weston

The Red Knight in Milan

I said to somebody at one time, 'If I had somebody to go with, I'd go to Milan' and we're talking about in the days when it was very, very unusual to travel away to see a football match. Well, about a week before the game, this chap rang me up and said 'I've got two tickets for the Milan game'. I couldn't believe it! At the time I was working at Bibby's and I had to get a passport pretty quickly, pretty sharpish, and off we went to Milan. One of the things which I always remember was being stuck at the end of the runway on this Britannia that was taking us to Milan. While the engine was revving up ready to take off, if you looked at the wings, then you could see that they were actually vibrating. I thought to myself, this plane isn't going to get to Milan. Anyway, we did get to Milan, and the thing was, I always remember, there was a fellow there on the plane, and he'd gone to enormous length to make himself a set of knight's armour of cardboard – it was

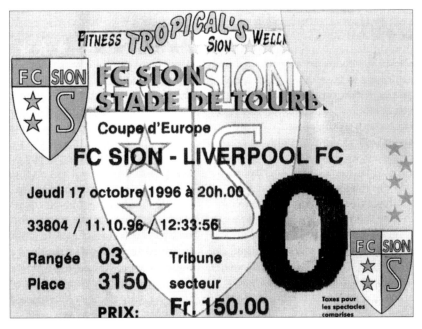

Match ticket for the game against FC Sion.

The ticket for the European Cup Final against Real Madrid in the Parc des Princes, Paris, Wednesday 27 May 1981. Liverpool won 1-0.

painted red all over. He sat with this on the plane and he had one of those big lances, you know, with a Liverpool flag on the end. When we touched down in Milan, they literally had to carry him off the plane. And later there he was waiting for the bus, you know, in the middle of the siesta hour, shouting and chanting, nobody taking a blind bit of notice. Anyway, we got this bus and ended up in The Palace. This, without doubt, is just about the most superb hotel in Milan that you could ever go to. But here again – and I couldn't believe it – there was a fellow in a pair of heavy corduroy trousers, with a red and white scarf on and a red hat on, and he goes into the cocktail bar in The Palace, Milan, and says to the barman, he says, 'Have you got a pint?' Well of course they didn't serve such things at the cocktail bar in Milan, you know. Funnily enough, it was the same hotel the Milan team were using. The tickets that we had allowed us to sit anywhere in the stadium that we wished. For some unknown reason, I think partly because we were encouraged to do so by the police, we sat behind the goal at one end. We got beat and Shankly was absolutely distraught. He was distraught because of one incident in particular. One of their players actually kicked the ball out of Tommy Laurence's hand, and scored. Then there was another goal which was blatantly offside – and both goals stood! There was no way back from that, but the impression I got was, to be quite honest with you, that the grass was too long for Liverpool. It might sound silly to suggest that the grass was too long, but we certainly were a yard short on the night, there was no doubt of that. The next day when we were actually being ferried by bus into the airport to come home to Speke, they made a roll call of the people. There were two people missing, but the travel agent didn't even get concerned about it. He simply said 'Oh, no' he said, 'We won't see them again. If you want to leave the U.K. with no trace that you'd ever left the U.K., then this is the way to do it.' This incident has always stood out in my mind, nothing to do with football, but I've always remembered it. Anyway, as I say, we came back, and we didn't win on that occasion, but that was the Milan game.

Harold S. Scott

'Lunch over Amsterdam'

In the very early days of European football, the club always chartered special flights to take players, directors and other senior officials to away games. I remember one game in particular, when we were scheduled to fly over to Amsterdam. Even before the plane started to taxi down the runway the champagne corks were popping, and everybody was enjoying themselves. As we were taking off, we were served more champagne – in fact, there was as much as you could drink. Then, when we reached level flight, an excellent three-course dinner was served. However, before we had time to finish our meals, the plane was starting to make its initial descent into Amsterdam. Realising the situation, one of the flight stewardesses alerted the pilot. Thirty seconds later he made the following announcement over the public address system, 'I believe that most of you are still enjoying your dinner. I'll circle over the airport for the next twenty minutes, to give you time to finish!' This he duly did and we touched down, replete, some thirty minutes later. I can't recall the score, but what a dinner!

Ken Davies

I had to tell my Scouse friend that it wasn't the Germans who were responsible for the Coliseum looking like this!

How Did the Coliseum End Up Like This?

In 1977 we flew out to Rome to see Liverpool play Borussia Mönchengladbach in the final of the European Cup. On the way out we met some Scousers who were based in Germany. The Aer Lingus jet that we flew out on was called the Saint Patrick. The whole experience was so amazing I'll never forget it for the rest of my life. We went along to see the sights of the ruins of the Coliseum. These two Scousers tagged along with us. It was clear that they'd never ventured much further than the outskirts of town. When they saw the Coliseum they were outraged and asked if it was the Germans who had done the damage during the war!

June Titherington

A Day Out in Paris

And then there was the time when we were in Paris in 1981. I got there – me and a couple of the lads. It was an evening match, so we got there early in the morning. We went out for lunch on the Champs-Élysées, gave the order in and we had a nice, easy half a bottle of wine each, to be sensible. But the waiter made an error and at the end of the meal he let us have another half bottle of wine each which we then had to consume of course – we couldn't leave that! So we thought that we'd have a little walk up to the match – on the map it only looked about a mile and a half away. As it happens it was a bit longer than that but on the way there were a few alehouses. So we went in

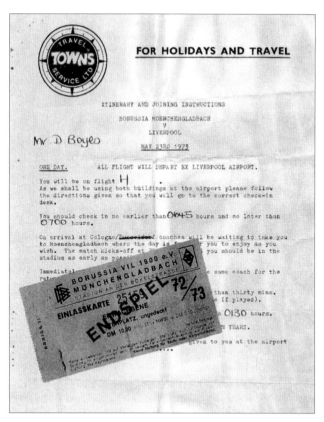

Left: Flight schedule for the game against Borussia Mönchengladbach – 23 May 1973. Unfortunately, we lost that particular game 2-0, but, as we'd won at Anfield earlier in the month 3-0, we won 3-2 on aggregate and went through.

Below: Ivy May and friends with their bold banner.

most of them, just for a swift half you understand, and at the end of the road my head was swimming. By this time, my only thought was, 'Whatever I do now, I mustn't lose the ticket'. So I held it in my fist all the way to the game. God knows how I lost it. We arrived at the entrance and, lo and behold, no ticket! I was hauled out of the line by a lad about eight-foot high with a machine gun. I think he was wondering what was happening, so then I thought, 'I'll give him some money'. So I gave him a hundred francs. He was happy with that and shoved me in. I never managed to see any of the first half, the alcoholic haze hadn't evaporated, but I was able to watch the second half in slow motion. There was a lad sitting in front of us with a flag, a massive one on a heavy pole, and he was moaning throughout the second half, 'We're going to get beat. Laurie Cunningham's going to score' – he just wouldn't let it go. Anyway, nine minutes from the end up rose Alan, slots it in and I then leap up, nick the lad's massive flag, and smash him over the head with it, at which point I then fell and rolled down about half a dozen steps! Because I'm round now and I haven't altered my shape really, it was okay – I just rolled. He was looking round for whoever had smashed him over the head, but I'd rolled out of his way, and he couldn't find me. Anyway, that was the end of that. We won 1-0. When we arrived at the hotel it was still only half-past eleven. All of a sudden, it dawned on us that we'd just won the European Cup, so we decided to go out again and celebrate. I suppose my last memory of that night would be the scene in a little bar having a ham sandwich – it wasn't really a ham sandwich, but a horrible hard French loaf, which was obviously three days old. I ended up throwing lumps of it at the waiter's head as he was going past. I can't remember getting back to the hotel, but that was a nice middle of the week excursion. When I got home I actually watched the match for the first time on video – it was very interesting.

David Pennington

£99 for the Trip of a Lifetime

My daughter got these tickets, £99 for each of us, that included the price of £3 for the game itself. We started off from Skelhorne Street, five National coaches, and there was a real sense of excitement and almost triumph – people were waving us off and cheering as the buses pulled out of the coach station. We were sleeping out of suitcases, but nobody seemed to mind. On the first night we stayed in France and the next morning we set off early to Switzerland. The following day we were aiming for Florence. It was a five-day tour, so we covered some miles during that time. On the day we got to Florence, we didn't stay that long, as we then had to set off for Rome. We arrived early in the morning. It was absolutely magnificent. All the German supporters were there, arriving in their super-deluxe coaches, and we were in our somewhat less-grand National coaches, but that didn't seem to matter to anyone. Anyway, there was much banter between the rival fans, but it was all very good-natured. We went to the Trevi Fountains, and many fans were splashing around, taking the opportunity of cooling themselves down. A German came over to me, and we got into quite a long conversation. He assured me that his team was going to win. I didn't share this view. He suggested that, irrespective of the outcome, we should have a drink after the game.

Match programme for the game against FC Sion.

We went our separate ways, he to his end of the ground and us to the other. We walked along as a group and, right in the middle of the group, was Bill Shankly himself. He was just like one of us. One of the supporters had lost his money. When Shanks heard this he gave him a few bob for himself. It was a little intimidating in the ground. At our end there were soldiers and police with guns. There were also several very large dogs, to say nothing of the heavy mesh wire which penned us in – almost like wild animals. There was just no need for it. Anyway, the game kicked-off, and it was very exciting game. It was just unbelievable! When we finally left the ground, it was decided that, instead of staying in Rome, we should make our way to Switzerland and do our celebrating there. We had a ball that night. We were one big happy family. From what I can gather, people who travelled either by train or jet didn't have such a good time as we did.

Ivy May

Lobster in Lisbon

In Lisbon I blotted my copybook. It was pouring with rain and I'd been at the stadium – it's called the Sun and Light, or something like that – all day. The stands themselves consist of a series of numbered cement steps on which you're supposed to sit. After a full day's work at the stadium and getting wringing wet into the bargain, I couldn't face the prospect of returning there for the game that evening, just to sit on a wet concrete step in the pouring rain. Earlier in the day I'd spotted a fish restaurant which looked particularly appealing, so when the coach called at the hotel, I did a bunk!

There were no loos at the ground when we played against FC Sion. We were given pass-outs.

While the match was on, I was sat in this lovely warm, dry restaurant eating the most delicious fresh lobster! The problems started when I got back to the hotel. The club secretary – at that time it was Peter Robinson – had noticed that I wasn't at the game. When he found out just where I'd been, he stated, in very clear and unequivocal English, that that would be the last time that I'd travel abroad with Liverpool – but it wasn't!

Ken Davies

Off to Switzerland

We went to a game at Anfield and we were in one of the hospitality suites. It was great, but quite a few of the people in there were only going for the booze and the free meal – they're not really football supporters. Well, after this game, we got talking and Ken said that he'd never been to a game in Europe and that he really would like the experience. Some few months later, Liverpool were scheduled to play one of the Swiss teams and Ken said that that was the game that we were going to! He, somehow, managed to get tickets and we were going to fly over just for the game. But, as we both agreed, doing it that way we would only see the game, we wouldn't be able to absorb any of the atmosphere or enjoy the game as we should, as we would be thinking about getting back to the airport and then back to work. The flight was due to touch down at four, the game was at eight and the flight home was leaving at midnight. That wasn't what we wanted. We decided it would be better, and cheaper, if we went by car. So, on the Wednesday night after we'd

Getting through the security at the FC Sion game.

The Liverpool supporters' area at FC Sion.

finished work, three of us set off for Switzerland. Peter was the third member of our group. We picked him up on the way down the M6.

As it happens, we had some business in Switzerland anyway and our contact there, an Englishman, phoned to say that he had got some tickets for us. We got rid of the first lot of tickets. We went whizzing down the M1, hoping to catch an early shuttle, when, all of a sudden, Ken pulled off the motorway, drove down some country lanes, in the middle of nowhere, and ended up at this absolutely fantastic pub. We had a few pints there and then said that we would have to be moving on. The manager asked us where we were travelling to and we said that we were going to Switzerland for a football match which was to be played the next day. Strange to say, he just didn't believe us! We left and caught the shuttle over in the middle of the night. We drove hard through France, and got to Switzerland. Before we arrived in Geneva, there was a viewing point, where you could look right over the lake. It was a fantastic view. We decided to take some photographs here and, to link it in, we unfurled our Liverpool banner, so it would add to the backdrop against the lake. Well, the people on the motorway just couldn't believe it, seeing this huge Liverpool banner framed against their wonderful lake. I'm sure that one or two nearly crashed as they took time to read what was written on the banner – remember, they had to translate as well as read!

We met Phil when we arrived and he'd booked us into this fantastic hotel. We had a shower and a little rest and then it was time for a few 'bevies'. We ventured out onto the town and asked a few people where the bars were. Nobody seemed to know, it was just as if it was wrong to be seen drinking alcohol in a public place. We wandered around for some time, and people seemed to be pointing us in a certain direction towards the other end of town. After quite a search, we eventually found this bar – but it was a milk bar! There was a selection of tea, coffee, milk or several different types of lemonade. We were informed, however, that there was an Irish pub about five minutes walk away called Jameson's. We walked along the main street in the general direction where we thought that this pub was located and, after some searching, we found it. Walking in, we ordered a few beers and asked if they had anything to eat. We were given three pies, one each that is, and they were absolutely great. Five minutes later, we ordered another three beers and another three pies. By this time we had quite a gathering around us. They couldn't get over these three Englishmen drinking beer and eating pies. The manager of the pub, who himself was an Irishman, told us that men only came here to get out of the house. They didn't drink beer like they do in England or Ireland, they order tea or coffee, and sit around and discuss all of the cares of the world. There's never very much beer sold, even though they have the best Guinness in Geneva. He went on to say that there's a lot of Irish people living in Geneva, but for some reason, they tended not to go out too often. We were invited back to the pub after the game, when the manager said that he would invite some of his friends around and we would have a bit of a party. He seemed fed-up with the fact that his pub was being used as a doctor's surgery. All they seemed to discuss was their ailments, the ailments of their pets, the state of their marriages or the state of the economy. They never seemed to be enjoying themselves.

We went along to the game and sat in just about the best seats in the ground. We were sat in between the European officials on one side, and the directors of Liverpool Football Club on the other. The seats were so different from what we were used to at Anfield – they were plush leather! At half time, we decided that, even though we were in such illustrious company, it was time to unfurl our banner again. We unfurled the banner right along the back of the stand all twenty foot of it. Well, the Swiss just couldn't believe what was happening, but they didn't seem to mind. They took it all in good part. There was a constant stream of fans, from both Switzerland and England taking shots of this fantastic banner which we'd brought all the way over from Blighty. At half time it was the hospitality thing, so we went down to this big room where there was loads of food and drink. There was so much it was untrue. We ate and drank for twenty minutes, and then it was time for the second half. We'd drunk so much, we didn't feel like going back, but we did want to see how Liverpool would get on in the second half. As we were making our way back, I tried once again to get a match programme, but they were all sold out. Just then, I saw the box where all the radio and press people were sitting and I happened to see Jim Beglin. He was reporting the game for Radio City. Without more ado, I introduced myself to him, the alcohol no doubt giving me more than a little Dutch courage, and asked if I could give a message to the folks back in Liverpool. I was live on the radio for a few minutes and, when I was leaving, I asked Jim for his programme. He was so taken aback that he handed me the programme without a second thought, and then signed it as well!

When we got back to the pub after the game, it was full of invited guests and we were the guests of honour. Nothing was too much for us to ask. We certainly enjoyed every minute whilst we were in there. We were drinking Baileys and pints of Guinness – what a mixture but it seemed to be going down very well. So much so, that we decided to go onto a club after that. We didn't look like the average football fan, in that, on this occasion, we were dressed in shirts and ties and all the gear. We were told that there

David Boyes' Dad – taken in Sapphire Street, Old Swan, Liverpool, on 30 May 1984; the day that Liverpool won the European Cup.

was a very good club just over the railway bridge, going out of town. We were also told that it was a little expensive, but by this time, we weren't that bothered anyway. We walked up to the club, and just about managed to get in. Although it was called a club, it was really like a very high-class brothel. We weren't bothered about the other attractions of the club, but we did want a drink. Instead of ordering champagne, which was the drink that seemed to be on most of the tables, we ordered three beers. We were given a choice, and ordered what we thought would be the cheapest drinks. The bill for our three drinks was presented as the drinks themselves were brought to our table. The bill for three halves of lager was forty-five pounds! We couldn't believe it. The bouncer took pity on us and brought over three more drinks which were 'on the house' – he quite obviously realised that we weren't going to be spending money on the other house attractions on that particular evening. We drank our 'freebie' beer and left.

Paul Stewart

A Black Eye for My Troubles

I was sitting in the house with my dad when Liverpool where playing in Rome against Borussia Mönchengladbach in the Final of the European Cup. Dad was an invalid, he only had one leg, so he had to use walking sticks. At halftime we were winning 1-0. Dad needed to take frequent exercise, so he was up on his walking sticks just walking around whilst he was watching the match. A few minutes into the second half and Simonsen smashed an equaliser for Borussia Mönchengladbach. I shut my eyes and dad, in anger, smashed his right-hand stick on the floor. The rubber end on the stick

All the Reds from Fazakerley were there.

After the long journey from Liverpool to Paris some refreshment was well-deserved!

Above left: Liverpool fans arriving in Paris – the coaches parked on one of the avenues leading from the Arc de Triomphe.

Above right: Guess where we're playing tonight!

made it rebound, and it hit me in the eye. So, not only had Simonsen equalised, but I'd got a black eye for my troubles. But, all's well that ends well, we won the game and with it the European Cup – but that game will live long in my memory.

David Pennington

Our Jumbo Jet to Europe

When we went to Liverpool's first European Cup Final, everything was chaotic – everything was booked up. There was no way that you could get a flight or a train ticket. In the end, Aer Lingus laid on another jumbo and we were lucky enough to get seats on that. We made it into a bit of a holiday, as did many other fans. We stayed there for three or four days – it was great. I've never ever had such a fantastic experience in my life. It wouldn't matter if Liverpool played in the final every year, that first year could never be bettered or repeated. Everything about it was surreal, even events such as when the players went to the Vatican. When we got to the ground itself, it was just a mass of red and white – you've never seen anything like it. It was overwhelming. What an atmosphere – you couldn't have bought it, it was priceless!

When we were coming back, we met a lad of thirteen on the jet. He'd got to Rome, gone to the game, and was now coming back in our jet. He didn't have a passport, he didn't have a ticket for the game, he had no money, and he certainly didn't have a ticket for the flight home, but there he was large as life. I just can't understand it. I can understand grown men selling their golf clubs or even their cars to get to the game, but I still can't understand how this thirteen year-old did that lot!

Paul Parry

Coupe des Clubs
Champions
Européens 1984/85

Europese Beker der
Landskampioenen
1984/85

FINALE

LIVERPOOL F.C.
JUVENTUS F.C.

29.5.1985 - 20.15
Stade du Heysel - Bruxelles
Heizelstadion - Brussel

Programme officiel   40 BF
Officieel programma

Match programme for the Heysel game.

The Red Fire Engine in Paris

Every year we used to go over to Boulogne to get some wine. It became a bit of a charity 'do' and one of my more affluent friends used to take over his red fire engine as a bit of a spectacle. One year, the year that Liverpool were playing in the Cup Final in Paris, my friend just couldn't be persuaded to carry on as far as Paris so that we could see the match – he wasn't that interested in football. Well, we really wanted to be there, so early the next morning we 'borrowed' the fire engine and drove off to Paris. What a stir we caused, driving up the Champs-Élysées in this red British fire engine – the Parisians had never seen anything like it before! We went to the game and got back to Boulogne as soon as we could. Unfortunately, my friend wasn't too pleased. I haven't been back for any more wine since!

Terry Murphy

A Worrying Night on Holiday

In early summer of 1985 we – that is my wife Edie and myself – took a small cottage in Stow-on-the-Wold for a short, and much-needed holiday. It had been some little while since we'd been able to go away for a few days and get away from it all and Stow-on-the-Wold was a village that we'd both always dreamed about seeing. We left at the weekend to make the long drive down in fact, it was the same time as our son, David,

David's Heysel ticket.

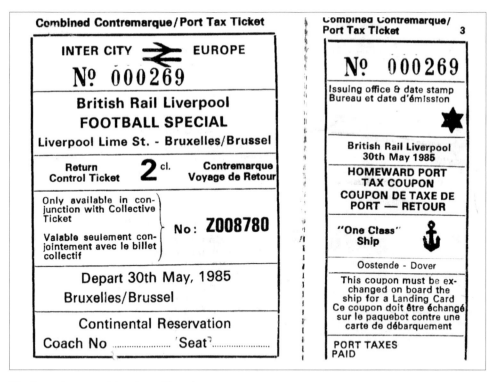

The home journey ticket from Heysel.

Jubilant fans after the 1977 European Cup Final.

was setting off for Brussels to see Liverpool play in the European Cup Final. He'd watched Liverpool in all of the other rounds, and now they were in the final against Juventus.

The morning of Wednesday 29 May dawned and it was sunny and bright. We decided to go out for the day and absorb the countryside in the area around Stow-on-the-Wold. We returned to the cottage later that evening, after what had been a very pleasant day's drive. When we put the TV on, we were shocked at the scenes which we were seeing coming from the Heysel Stadium – we just couldn't believe it, no doubt like millions of other viewers up and down the country. We tried phoning the local police station, but there was no answer. In desperation we drove down, but the station was shut for the night. We found out that, with all of the cutbacks, the local police station was now only open during peak times in the day. By now however, there was a telephone number being flashed on the screen which people could phone for information. We tried to get through all night – literally – but the lines were engaged all of the time. By eight o'clock the next morning, we still didn't know whether or not David was okay. Eventually, at some time after ten in the morning, the owner of the cottage phoned us and said that David had managed to contact him and that he was alright. The sheer relief completely overwhelmed us. It's a night that I don't often think about, but when I do, it's always with an immense sense of thankfulness and relief.

George 'Bob' Stowell

Another Great Red Day

I was fifteen and it was the European cup Final in 1977. At that time we lived in Banbury Avenue, which was a street – it wasn't a terraced street, they were all semi-detached houses with garages, blocks of garages. Right up the street we had the tables laid out and the only recollection of seeing something like that before, was when my mum turned round and said that there was the Queen's Jubilee when everybody had street parties. The English Rose was the main pub in our neighbourhood, just at the top of Mackets Lane – all the men were in there. It was great, there was a real carnival atmosphere. There were loads of banners with 'Liverpool FC' written all over and I'm saying to myself, 'What happens if we lose?', and the reaction was that we'd have a great party anyway, we've got to the final, but even so everybody was saying, 'But we won't lose!'– people were so confident of Liverpool winning. Nobody seemed to bother what was going on around them, we were all eating pies and there were Cokes and things like that for the kids and we were all running up the street and kicking balls and then we just ran into the pub at the top of the road. And in the pub, they used to have these turnstile-type doors and we were all running in and out of them. Well, if you ran in and out of them at any other time you'd get kicked out by the manager, but this time everybody was grabbing hold of us and giving us drinks and everybody in the pub was singing traditional Liverpool songs like Walk On. In fact, we must have been in the pub until ten o'clock that night, all walking around and recalling the final score. I can't remember everything, being only a kid, but thinking on now, I wonder if there was the odd Evertonian shouting the odd bit of abuse – but there wasn't! Nobody said one bad

Liverpool fans by the Arc de Triomphe, Paris.

thing, it was just Liverpool, Liverpool, Liverpool, everything and everybody was red that day. That was a really great experience.

Mark Rochford

Rome 1977

Apart from the '65 Cup win, when the Liver birds didn't fly away, I think that the most memorable game for me was the '77 European Cup Final in Rome. If you look back over the last twenty-five years, that is probably the best footballing final of all of them. The game had everything. It was lovely and warm – we were all in shirtsleeves, you were with all of your friends, we were a goal up and we were coasting it. All of a sudden Simonson scored with a wonderful goal and, seconds afterwards, Clemence had to make the save of the match. We'd gone from the highest plateau to crossing our legs, crossing our feet, our arms were crossed – we just didn't want to watch! Thankfully McDermott popped up, he scored a goal, a fine goal. Then Smithy got one and finally Neal took the penalty. In the end it looked like the easiest game of the season I would think. It was soured for me, however, because at that time I was working in Manchester. I used to travel to Manchester every day and the guy with whom I worked was a fanatical United supporter. We also won the League that season

The official UEFA souvenir programme for the European Cup Final held in Rome on Wednesday 30 May 1984.

and we went to Wembley and lost to two fluke goals. Harry always used to say, 'Never mind whether they were flukes or not, look at the book. Who won the Cup?' This caused a little aggravation, but you can't have too much aggravation if the guy's your boss. I then took time off work to go to Rome. When I came back, we'd won two out of three – I was happy.

Alan Reason

A Remarkable Meeting

Liverpool drew Cologne, but there was no away goals counting double. Liverpool played in Cologne first, and got a 0-0 draw, and we were very happy about that. When they came back to Anfield to play the second leg, it was also a 0-0 draw, so it went on to a third game – Amsterdam, I think it was. And in the third game, Liverpool went into a 2-0 lead, but then Cologne got back with two goals, so it finished up 2-2. There was extra time and in the end they had to toss with a disc. The referee tossed the disc, and on the first toss it, stuck in the mud. So there'd been three draws and even tossing the coin didn't settle the game, it just stuck, edge-on. Anyway, they had to toss it again, and Liverpool won on the next toss. But I remember those games because I went with this mate of mine, Tom Swinnerton, and decided to queue in the Kemlyn Road, and we were facing towards the Kop. The queue was going up to the Kop end, right up Kemlyn Road, down again to the bottom, back up to the top, and so on, and the police were controlling all this. We got in the queue early, and we spent our time going up the road and down again. However, what was happening was people were coming up to the top and instead of going all the way down back again, they were nipping across the end to cut out a complete leg – we did it too actually. We thought that we were pretty good doing that! Anyway, the police lost control, and the whole of Kemlyn Road suddenly became one queue, from the houses on one side to the houses on the other – a solid queue all the way down to the Kop. So, in the crush and hurly-burly I lost touch with this mate of mine, but I got within sight of the Kop gates, in fact I got within probably about fifteen yards. We had to home in onto perhaps four gates, or something like that, and we weren't making any progress. The people in the centre were the best, but people on the outside were just being forced out all the time. This went on for quite a while, and in the end I just walked out of the queue. I just walked out of it altogether and stood on the other side of the main road, just looking at the whole road seething with people, all fighting to get in these gates, and I thought to myself, 'This is bloody stupid, it's really stupid this' and I was really annoyed. I thought that I was wasting my time. Anyway, when I was standing there, round the corner on the main road, I noticed a single gate with nobody there at all, and my first thoughts were, 'Well that can't possibly be open, with all these people around the corner, fighting to get into four gates, and here's one around the front with not a soul there.' I think it was now past kick-off time, and it had started snowing as well, so I just thought to myself, 'Well, I don't believe that I'm going to get into that gate, but I'll try anyway.' So I walked across the road, and there was a fellow behind the counter, so I just paid and just walked in – I just couldn't believe it! Anyway, I made my way up the steps of the Kop, and it was pretty full then, so I decided to go down a bit towards the pitch. So I muscled my way in and I was standing there looking at my watch and I just looked at the bloke next to me and it was this mate of mine, Tom Swinnerton! We looked at each other and we couldn't believe it. We had lost each other easily an hour before, and then we just turned up alongside of each other. It was incredible, we just couldn't believe it. As it happens, the game was called off anyway, after all that the game was cancelled! They made an announcement and said that they'd give out vouchers. So on the way out you had to queue again, to get your voucher. We'd had enough by that stage – so we just walked out and left it. I didn't go to the game, but I believe that it was a really good game. Liverpool were tremendous and they had a goalie who played an absolute blinder – he saved everything.

The game finished 0-0 again.

Jack London

CHAPTER 6

SHANKLY

Shankly's Arrived!

And then we came into the Bill Shankly era when it all changed. I'm talking about the period where people if you like, had absolute intensity for what they were doing, I mean, I don't think in those days anybody would have ever thought of cheating in the game, I don't think it entered anybody's mind to cheat or to bet on a game or to throw a game or anything of that nature. People, the people playing the game in those days, were a different class of person. I think that when Bill Shankly came to Liverpool, he brought an absolute honesty which had rarely existed before. It was a question of right mental attitude as far as Shankly was concerned, you had to be absolutely and totally honest and dedicated to what you were doing and the stories are legion about Shankly and his attitude towards players. I can remember the first thing he did when he came to Liverpool, he brought into the club St John, the centre forward, and then he brought in Rowdy Yeats and then he brought in Tommy Laurence the goalkeeper, and he built a team around those three people. And I always remember that at that time, we had started to do things on an international level as regards Liverpool. This had never even been imagined before, but it was then, for instance, that money started to come into the game. Money started to dictate, but Shankly never allowed it at Liverpool. We had a lot of good players at Liverpool at that time. We had Ian Callaghan, the outside left, we also bought in Gordon Milne, if you remember. One of the things that Shankly did, was to always carry an extra half-back in his team and that was Gordon Milne's role, in as much as he was on the team sheet at outside left, but in actual fact he had a roving commission. Essentially he was an extra half-back. It was four across the back wasn't it in those days and that was the pattern upon which Shankly and Paisley eventually built their success.

Harold S. Scott

Shankly's First Game as Manager

And then they brought the other fellow in, the Shankly fellow. The first game that he was in charge at Anfield we were playing Cardiff City. He'd been appointed on the Wednesday of that week and we were due to play Cardiff on the Saturday. I don't know whether he'd picked the team or not, or whether he'd been involved with the

Above: 'Bill Shankly – This is Your Life'. The Liverpool manager is grabbed by Eamonn Andrews on arrival at Euston Station.

Right: Liverpool players celebrating the 1974 FA Cup victory.

selection at all, but the net result was that we got turned over, losing 5-1. By the end of the game the crowd were chanting, 'We want a manager, we want a manager' – and this was his first-ever match! But that seemed to do it – he took to them and that made for the initial bond. He took to Anfield there and then.

Gerry Tyrrell

The Japanese Rolls-Royce

Shanks was due to pick up a new car, a Nissan Sunny, one of the first cars of its kind in Liverpool. I didn't know much about these cars, as we'd only taken delivery of a few up until that time. Shanks came along with Nessie and took delivery of the car. He seemed very pleased, but I was a little apprehensive, as it was a completely new car to us in the garage. He left, apparently very pleased with his new toy. However, five minutes later, the phone was ringing and our telephonist said that it was Mr Shankly and he wanted to speak with me very urgently. I feared the worst, thinking that the car must have broken down a few minutes out from the garage – nothing could have been further from the truth. When I took the call, I was greeted by a jubilant Bill Shankly, who informed me, in very colourful English, that I'd just sold him 'A ******* Japanese Rolls-Royce.' As they say in footballing circles – he was over the moon!

Jeff Tinnion

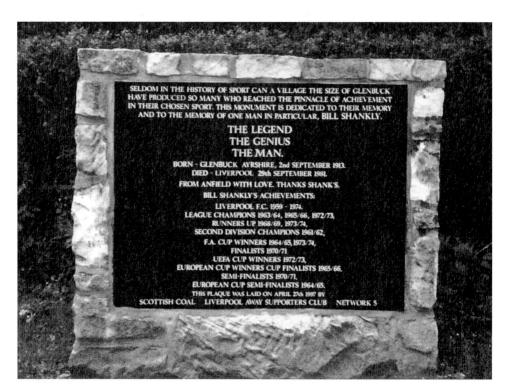

The Shankly Memorial, Glenbuck.

Glenbuck

Glenbuck is a little mining village in Scotland, not so very far from Ayr racecourse. That mightn't be too significant in itself, but what is of far greater significance, is the fact that in 1913 Bill Shankly was born there. The local football team was called the Glenbuck Cherry Pickers, but Shankly never actually played for them. A monument was built in the village and dedicated to all of the footballers from the village – and there were many. It's amazing to think that from such a small village, there should be so many of the young men sign as professional football players. There's not much left of the village now, except for two houses – one owned by a local coal merchant and the other owned by a little old lady who lives on her own, but it's become something of a shrine for Liverpool supporters. It's strange when you go there, there's a sort of eerie feeling as you get there. It's very real. It's just about possible to make out where the old footy pitch was, but that's about all.

Paul McEvoy

Starting to Sort Things Out

Shankly came to a team that was a Second Division team in a Third Division ground, and that's the best way you can describe Anfield at the time. For instance, the Anfield Road end was simply a wooden stand – just a wooden stand. It was a joke! The first thing Shankly did was to get rid of that and he lifted the club from there. When he first went to Melwood, he couldn't believe the lack of facilities for training. He also couldn't believe that the players only used to train for three mornings a week and go home at half-past eleven. He wasn't going to have that and he started to sort everything out from there!

Gerry Tyrrell

Shanks Sent Me a Ticket

I'm often reminded about what a great man Shanks was. In 1974 I was struggling to get a ticket for the Cup Final. All of my mates had managed to get tickets, but I couldn't get one for love or money. I was hoping that this was going to be my first final. I'd tried everything, but all to no avail. One Friday night, Bill Shankly wrote an article in the Liverpool Echo, saying that he would help any genuine fans who were having difficulty in obtaining tickets. I told my dad that, as a last desperate attempt, I intended writing to Mr Shankly. I bought a pound postal order and placed it in a stamped addressed envelope. Time passed and no ticket was received, but then one day, just before the final, I received my letter from Mr Shankly with a ticket inside. I couldn't believe my eyes when I saw not just the ticket for the final, but also a note on headed notepaper saying, 'Best Wishes B Shankly.' I still treasure it to this day.

David Boyes

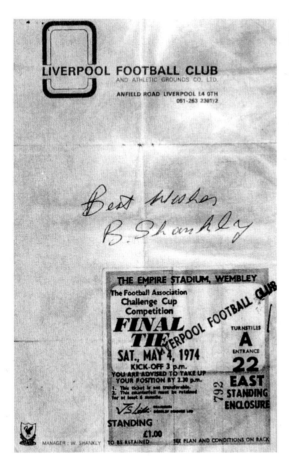

The ticket that Bill Shankly sent to David Boyes.

Can You Have Him Ready for Saturday?

It was a Tuesday and already late into the day, when Shanks brought one of his players into the clinic for an examination of a knee injury. The player was already using crutches and had his leg bound from ankle to thigh with woollen bandages to protect a very swollen knee joint. Ever the optimist, Mr Shankly was heard to say, 'Can you have him ready for Saturday, he's a very important member of the team' – he didn't make it!

Frank McCormack

The Liverpool Pattern

On the football side, I always remember talking to him one day about the famous Liverpool pattern and where he got the idea from. I can never remember the name of the guy, he was Hungarian, and his name was something like Pimpernel, he was a Hungarian coach, and he showed Shanks this method – 'Pass the ball, support your mate; pass the ball, support your mate.'

Jeff Tinnion

Even the Width of the Pitch is Important

Shankly used to come here quite often before setting off for football matches. Later on, after he'd parted company with Liverpool Football Club, he took to going down to Wrexham quite a lot. He always reckoned that the ground at Wrexham was quite considerably wider than most grounds in the Football League. He even proffered some information regarding the tactics that should be adopted on such grounds in order to gain the best advantage. It's alleged that, whilst Shankly was still at Liverpool, Brian Clough had the playing area at Forest narrowed to see if this could help them beat Liverpool.

Paul Parry

A Good Square Meal – Courtesy of Mr Shankly

I often used to go abroad in the summer with my tent and sleeping bag and trot here, there and everywhere, and frequently, on my way home I would call in at Liverpool's pre-season friendlies in various countries: Germany, Belgium and several other countries. One time I'd been with a friend and we'd hitch-hiked down to Greece and we camped on a couple of Greek islands and then we set off to come back via Brussels where Liverpool were due to play in a pre-season friendly. So we arrived in Brussels and got to the campsite. After sorting that out, I decided to go for a wander around the

A LEGEND IN HIS OWN TIME

BILL SHANKLY
Manager, Liverpool Football Club,
12th December, 1959 — 12th July, 1974.
A TRIBUTE

Best Wishes
Bill Shankly

This Book is Copy number

1160

of a Limited Edition of only
Two Thousand Five Hundred Copies

Certified.
on behalf of the Publisher,
J.H. LEEMAN LTD.
NESTON, MERSEYSIDE.
Printers of "A Legend in His Own Time"

As everybody knew – he really was a legend in his own lifetime.

town. For some reason which I can't remember, I happened to be on my own – she'd gone off to do something else. Anyway, I found the team, I found Shankly, or rather, he found me, and said that I was disturbing the team when they should be resting. He didn't seem to be too pleased, but he said, 'Meet me at the ground tomorrow, and I'll give you some tickets.' The next day we set off for the ground in good time and waited outside and there were quite a few other Liverpool fans there, which was quite usual for a pre-season friendly, when perhaps twenty or thirty people would just drop in as they do. So, the team arrived, and Shankly arrived, and he came straight over and gave tickets out to everybody who was there. That was the normal practice in those days. He looked at us, called us over and took us to one side. 'How are you two getting home?' he said in a very abrupt manner, which seemed to sound more brusque because of his heavy Scots accent – 'Oh, we're okay, we're hitchhiking' – 'Have you got enough money to get home? It's not right for lassies to be hitch-hiking.' – 'No, we're quite alright thank you Mr Shankly and thank you for the tickets' – 'Here, take this and make sure that you have a good meal before you set off for home' and he gave us some money. I can't remember how much it was, but it was certainly enough to get us a good meal and a little bit more besides. And that was just to make sure that two young girls, that he'd never met before, or was never likely to meet again, had a good square meal. I loved him before, and I loved him forever after that. He's my idol!

Marilyn Clay

Meeting Mr Shankly

I went to Saint Edward's School in Sandfield Park, Liverpool, and Mr Shankly lived quite near to the school as it happens. When he retired, he used to run around the school's pitches, just jogging around to keep himself fit. He got quite involved with the school, even having his car spayed in the school colours of purple! He also had a purple jogging suit. Every Tuesday we had to play at some sort of sport, but I wasn't the sporty type. With a few friends, I opted to go cross-country running, as it was called then. We used to set off from school at a reasonable pace, and when we were out of sight, we'd slow down to a gentle trot, or even walk around just chatting and collecting conkers. One day we saw this figure running towards us, so we too started to ease into a gentle run. When the figure caught up to us, it was Bill Shankly. He ran along by the side of us for some time, asking our names and extolling the virtues of the school. He also said that we should work hard if we wanted to succeed in life. He shook hands with all of us and then off he jogged. We met him on a few occasions after that, and he always inquired how we were doing.

Peter Moss

Shankly Lets Us In To See Wolves

It was the climax to the season, Liverpool needed to win this match to be Champions again, but if Wolves lost, it meant that they would be relegated. I travelled down from Barrow-in-Furness to Wolverhampton by minibus, hoping to get there in time for a few pre-match drinks. That idea soon went out of the window when I got to the ground and found it heaving with at least 20,000 other supporters who'd had the same idea as me. By six-fifteen, all hopes of getting into the ground vanished when the turnstiles were closed. Like thousands of others, I just walked around the ground in desperation – I even attempted to get into the Wolves end! It was now getting very close to kick-off time as I stood outside of the changing room. All of a sudden, one of the windows was opened, and out popped the familiar head of Tommy Smith. He shouted to somebody behind me, and indicated that he would try to get him into the ground. Whoever Tommy had been speaking to was now moving nearer to the changing room door. Not being slow on the uptake, I pushed myself forward and stood right behind him. The door was then opened for a period of no more than five seconds, and in that time, I managed to propel myself and this other character into the changing room. Molineux is a very old ground, and the facilities are not that good, but what struck me most was not that we were stood in the players' changing room as they were getting changed, but the fact that the changing room looked more like the one which I had been used to at school! The climax of the afternoon for me, however, was when the great man himself came along and directed the two of us to the players' tunnel. We sat near to the dugout for the whole of the game – it was magic! To end the season in style, and also as Champions of course, from going 1-0 down, we came back and won 3-1.

David Stowell

Stay Away From The Hookey Walla

Late nights and night clubs were an anathema to Mr Shankly where his players were concerned. He heard of a very popular night club, not too far away from Anfield, called 'The Wookey Hollow'. Advising his players one morning, he said 'Now boys, it's very important that you get to bed early and get your rest, and make sure that you stay away from The Hockey Walla'.

Frank McCormack

Mine's Two

Bill came along one day to collect a new car. He often came with his wife, Nessie, and she was with him on this occasion. As the trainee always makes the tea, Mike Hughes, our trainee at the time, came in with three piping hot cups of tea. He'd taken the precaution of asking how many sugars for each of us before coming back with the brew. Bill wanted one, Nessie wanted none, and there was to be two sugars in my tea. As it happens, Mike got the order mixed up and gave everyone the wrong cup – he really was very nervous in front of the great man. Realising his mistake just before he left the offices he turned and said to Mr Shankly that, instead of giving him the cup with just one sugar in, he'd actually given him the cup with two sugars in – quick as a flash, Shanks said to him, 'Don't worry laddie, I'll just drink the half!'

Jeff Tinnion

Shankly's Rage

This story is probably apocryphal, it's certainly very well-known on the Kop and throughout Anfield generally – but I'm going to tell it anyway. It's about the time at Melwood when, after a long and hard training session, the team were just getting ready to finish for the day. Bill Shankly had other ideas however, and suggested that they could end the session by playing a five-a-side game. Shankly was intensely competitive, and was always captain of one of the sides. Sometimes, when the players were feeling a little mischievous, they would either deliberately concede goals, or conversely, not allow goals to be scored. It all depended on the score at the time, and just how much they wanted to wind up the boss. On the occasion in question, the score was even. There was no way that Shankly was going to draw the game to an end before his team had taken the lead. The inevitable happened. A new signing, not being aware of the unwritten rules of these games, failed the read the subtle nuances and saved the ball from crossing the goal line. Shankly thought that the ball had crossed the line, and disputed the fact that the game would have to end in a draw. He was outraged, and fiercely continued to insist that the ball had actually crossed the line. Looking for some final judgement on the issue, he turned to the Liverpool captain, Phil Neal, who happened to be sitting on the sidelines. Now, Phil Neal had been a first team player for many years, he was also known to be a very quiet and retiring man – a very 'private' individual. Shankly asked for his verdict and agreed to abide by the decision. The reply didn't please him, as the ball was adjudged not to have crossed the line. In a fit of pique he was heard to exclaim, 'I don't know, he's been with us for almost seven years now and hasn't opened his mouth, and when he does we find out that the man's a *******
liar!'

Jason 'JC' Crewe

Some of Shankly's Signings

Then we bought the St John fellow. It was absolutely tremendous when they bought St John. People can argue and argue and argue about when it all began, but to me it began with the signing of St John. Of that, there's no doubt in my mind at all. A lot of people put it down to Yeats. Yeats was a great signing, but St John was charismatic, don't worry about that! St John was a charismatic figure, he was the flame that started the fire, don't worry about anybody else. Shankly bought great players. Shankly bought players that fitted into a pattern. Shankly bought the likes of Geoff Strong who was an Arsenal reserve. Shankly bought Geoff Strong because he knew that he could do a job for Liverpool. He also knew the mentality and ability of the players who would fit into the system. He knew exactly what he was buying. Shankly never bought a player that wouldn't do what needed to be done for Liverpool. He would buy a player out of the Third Division, or the Fourth Division even, if he knew he would do a job for Liverpool, vis-à-vis Keegan. Keegan was the classic example. He was a limited footballer, Keegan, don't worry about that. A great enthusiastic footballer, a self-made footballer, but Shankly saw him as a Liverpool footballer. He was a ninety-minute man who was going to give his best, no matter what.

Throughout his career at Liverpool, Shankly was noted for his shrewd signings.

Gerry Tyrrell

Mr Shankly Will Always Sign Autographs

Years ago, when I was about eleven or twelve I went down to Melwood to watch the team training. There were lots of other kids about. After we'd been watching for a little while, Bill Shankly came over. All the kids started shouting, 'Bill, can we have your autograph?' He didn't make any response. The groundsman, who was stood just behind me said, 'Call him Mr Shankly'. I shouted out, 'Can I have your autograph please Mr Shankly?' Straight away he came over and signed my book – I've still got that signature today.

Joe Sullivan

Eli's New Car

For years Eli Wass was the groundsman at Anfield and at this particular time he was looking for a new car – that is, new to him. He'd found out that Shanks was trading-in his car and thought that he might like to buy it – everyone worshipped Shanks. When he got to the garage, he couldn't quite meet the asking price. Shanks came in with his car a few days later and when I told him that Eli was interested but couldn't meet the price, Shanks gave me the difference in the trade-in. That was the kind of man he was. Later in the week Eli came along and said that he couldn't afford to buy the car. I told him about Shanks' gesture. He just couldn't believe it and actually broke down in tears. A few hours later he drove off a very happy man.

Jeff Tinnion

Why We Lost to Arsenal

Shanks always blamed himself when Liverpool lost to Arsenal in the 1971 Cup Final. If you look at any footage of that game, Liverpool were playing in long-sleeved shirts, and it was particularly hot that day. He maintained that if he'd have packed the silk shirts with the short sleeves, then it would have been a very different outcome.

Jeff Tinnion

November Droop

Eventually, when we first won the Cup, just before that we had a lot of young stars, they were getting married and, of course, they were marrying young fashion models and things like this. At that time, as today strangely, Liverpool, round about November, always went into a droop for some unknown reason. They seemed to have three weeks when they never won anything. Bill Shankly and Bob Paisley were very concerned about this. One Monday, or was it a Tuesday, morning at training, he called the players back in the afternoon – Liverpool normally only train in the morning. When the players got back to Melwood, because we'd bought Melwood by this time, Shankly was missing. What the players didn't know, was that Shankly had rounded up all their wives and had entertained them to lunch back at Anfield. Over lunch he took the opportunity of expressing his views on the situation and suggested that the reason for their lack of performance on the pitch, could be put down to the fact, for instance, that all his players had married these young models and things, and their minds were not really, shall we say, totally on playing football. He then suggested to them, for instance, that from Wednesday onwards, certainly from Thursday night onwards, they should deny their favours to their husbands, in as much as it was taking too much out of them. As far as he could see, that was the only thing that must have been interfering with his team winning – the fact, for instance, that they were being too liberal with their favours from Thursday night onwards before a game.

That story soon got round Liverpool, and it caused quite a lot of hilarity in actual fact. Nevertheless, we still to this day have a droop round about November which nobody really understands.

Harold S. Scott

Shanks Couldn't Stop Laughing

The biggest dinner we ever did was at the Crest in Runcorn, it was for Steve Heighway. I suggested that he should ask Shanks to be the after-dinner speaker. Shanks was pleased to oblige. On the night, I picked him up at six o'clock and, on the way over – we were driving down the 'Ford' Road at this time – he rehearsed his speech. Well, it was so funny, I just couldn't stop laughing. Then, because I was laughing, Shanks also started laughing. We just couldn't stop – we drove over the Runcorn Bridge 'in bulk'. As the great man got up to deliver his speech, every single person in the room stood up and raised their hands in the air – just like Shanks did himself, but this was in tribute to him.

Jeff Tinnion

CHAPTER 7

IN THE LEAGUE

On the Stroke of Time, Torres Scored the Winner

We'd joined a cruise going from Punta Arenas in Chile right down to the tip of Cape Horn, and then up to Ushuaia, which is the southern-most city in the world and very remote. We docked sometime on Saturday morning, 7 February 2009, the day that Liverpool were due to play Portsmouth down at Fratton Park.

After breakfast on the boat we were driven to our hotel for the night, before flying up to Buenos Aires the next day. As soon as we got to the hotel room I switched on the telly to check and see if, by any chance, the Liverpool match was being screened. Just as I managed to find the channel with the match on, Portsmouth scored due to an error by Reina; Portsmouth were now leading 2-1. I couldn't believe it. And, try as we might, we just couldn't equalise, that is right until the dying minutes of the game. With about ten minutes left we managed to get the ball up into the Portsmouth eighteen yard area, and Kuyt scored a very well worked goal from an extremely difficult angle. David James looked nonplussed, although in fairness, I don't think that he could have done much about it. Liverpool started pressing as much as they could to try to score the winner, but, without Steven Gerrard who had a hamstring strain, it proved somewhat difficult. It was horrible, knowing that we were going to settle, or rather, going to have to settle for just the one point when being at the top of the table is so critical, and of course, United had a game in hand. Fortunately, just on the stroke of time, Torres, ably assisted by Kuyt and one or two others, managed to score the winner. It was an excellent goal, and certainly as good as the goal which Kuyt had scored some ten minutes earlier. We couldn't believe that we'd actually managed to take all three points, although Liverpool obviously deserved all of them.

As soon as the game was over I phoned our son over in England; he too had watched the game and was very pleased and a little relieved to know that we were still sitting at the top of the table. After that we left the hotel to have a look around Ushuaia; right next to the hotel there was a very up-market sports shop, and bang in the very centre of the shop window was a Liverpool top! So, even in Tierra del Fuego, they have supporters of our glorious team.

David Paul

Above: At the start of the 1934/1935 season, Liverpool played Manchester City twice in a week, losing 3-1 away on 29 August, but then winning 2-1 at home on 5 September. Swift manages to save this header from Wright, with English there (on the left), just in case of a rebound.

Left: Still supporting down at Cape Horn.

We Were Poised to Take the Title

I went along to the last game of the '89 season, a very sad season for us after the disaster at Hillsborough. But, things had been going well on the field. In fact, we were poised to take the title at the end of the season if things went well against Arsenal. Everything *was* going well until Alan Hansen, one of my all-time favourites, just stood on the ball near to the end of the game, as if saying to the opposition, 'Come and get it if you can'. Just then, in one or two moves I hate to remember, Arsenal did get the ball and Michael Thomas, who was later to join our playing squad, ran down to the Anfield Road end with the ball and scored. As we came out of the ground, totally dejected after having given away the league title, a young lad, about twelve or thirteen, was crying his eyes out at the bottom of the stairs – I felt like crying too, and I'm sure that many other fans felt the same.

James Bennett

A Drubbing from Birmingham City

Birmingham City ended top of the league that season. They had a great side including England's goalkeeper, a fellow called Jeff Merrick. They also had England's right back, Jeff Hall. We went to watch Liverpool playing them at Birmingham. I was standing with a few mates of mine, and even quite early on in the game we were being beaten 1-0. The next thing Liddell makes it 1-1, and our prospects began to look a little better. Then Birmingham were awarded a penalty. Fortunately, we had Doug Rudham keeping goal for us. He was a South African amateur and had distinguished himself on a number of occasions in goal. For instance, he played a great game against Everton when we beat them 4-0. Anyway, the penalty was taken, and Dougie saved it. I turned around to one of my mates, and said, 'Do you know what, I think this is going to be our day.' The final score was 9-1, to Birmingham! At the end of the season, Leicester City and Birmingham City were slugging it out for the title, and Birmingham were due to play one of their last games at Anfield. In order to lift the title, Birmingham had to win this game, but Liverpool were anxious to avenge themselves from the 9-1 humiliation earlier in the season. The result was a 0-0 draw, so the Liverpool players were satisfied, and Birmingham failed to win the title.

Gerry Tyrell

Wolves '76

I think it all began for me when we were away to Wolves in 1976. It was the last match of the season and we had to either win or get a low draw. McClintock, who was the captain of Queens Park Rangers, was listening to the radio in London, and Wolves were winning 1-0. So, understandably, he thought that his team were going to win the league and he was made up. Then, with only fifteen minutes to go, up comes big Kevin and smashes in the equaliser! It wasn't a spectacular goal by any stretch of the imagination, but it won us the league. We went on to win that match 3-1, and that will never be erased from my memory. From that goal we won the league, and from that we went on to the St Etienne match, which everyone will remember. But, if we hadn't have equalised we wouldn't have won the league, and the St Etienne game wouldn't have happened. That's when it all began for me I think. Liverpool have played a huge part in that many peoples lives, and thinking about that game brings all the memories flooding back again.

David Pennington

When A. N. Other Played for Liverpool

One of the amusing events was during the latter years of the war. I was only a young boy at the time. Because most of the regular players were away on active service, and the Football League had been suspended as such, team sheets were often quite vague even until just before the game. We used to have players like Mullin from Wolves guesting for either Liverpool or Everton. On other occasions we'd have Notts County come up, and they'd have players in their team who were stationed near the club, and who would play for them on a game-by-game basis. The situation caused anomalies to appear in the matchday programme. Often, I noticed that A. N. Other was playing at outside left for Liverpool. My father tried to explain to me that his name wasn't really A. N. Other, but he couldn't get it through to me. I was convinced that I'd seen this A. N. Other playing, a superb player at outside left. It's funny to look back now, but of course, it's memories like that of which childhood fantasies are made.

Harold S. Scott

A brilliant shot from Wright, which sent Liverpool into the lead when they were playing Leeds United at Anfield on 18th March 1936. Liverpool won 2-1.

Derby Day '86

In 1986 we won the double. On derby day (Anfield), 22 April, my dad had a stroke. I spent all day with him in hospital. All afternoon he was asking the porters if there had been any score. We lost 2-0 that day. My dad said, 'We'll remember this day son'. We ended up eleven points behind Everton that day. 'Don't worry, we'll still win the League' he said. He died on 13 March, just six or seven weeks before we won the double. He would have been a proud man if he had lived.

I was lucky enough to get a ticket for the final that year, so I put a photograph of my dad on the front of my hat. In that way, my dad came with me to Wembley on that wonderful day.

David Boyes

Nottingham's a Long Way to Hitch-Hike

This happened about thirty-five years ago, when I was about eleven or twelve. Me and Terry Daracott, who went on to play for Everton, used to hitch-hike everywhere to watch Liverpool. On this particular Wednesday afternoon we sagged school and, in our little torn uniforms, we went down the road hitch-hiking our way to Nottingham. It was really difficult getting there, as there were no motorways in those days. Anyway, we did get there, no worries, robbing a few cakes here and there, we made our way, illegally, into the ground and got cut to pieces when we were climbing over the barbed wire. The first aid people came to our rescue and patched us up. So there we were, two rough kids from Liverpool watching Liverpool play at Nottingham from an extremely advantageous position. We levelled some abuse at the Nottingham players when we

LEAGUE FIXTURES.	LEAGUE FIXTURES.
1952.	**1953.**
Aug. 23—Preston N.E. ......Away	Jan. 3—Stoke City ....Away
,, 27—Sheffield Wed. ...Home	,, 10—F.A. Cup, 3rd Rd. ....
,, 30—Stoke City ....Home	,, 17—Manchester City Home
Sept. 3—Sheffield Wed. ...Away	,, 24—Portsmouth ......Away
,, 6—Manchester City Away	,, 31—F.A. Cup, 4th Rd. ....
,, 10—Tottenham H. ...Home	
,, 13—Portsmouth ......Home	Feb. 7—Middlesbrough ....Away
,, 15—Tottenham H. ...Away	,, 14—West Brom. A. ...Home
,, 20—Middlesbrough ...Home	,, 21—Newcastle U. ...Away
,, 27—West Brom. A. ....Away	,, 28—Bolton W. ....Home
Oct. 4—Newcastle U. ...Home	
,, 11—Bolton W. ....Away	Mar. 7—Aston Villa ......Away
,, 18—Aston Villa ......Home	,, 14—Sunderland ......Home
,, 25—Sunderland ......Away	,, 21—Wolverham't'n Away
Nov. 1—Wolverham't'n Home	,, 28—Charlton Ath. ...Home
,, 8—Charlton Ath. ...Away	
,, 15—Arsenal ....Home	Apr. 3—Cardiff City ......Home
,, 22—Derby County ...Away	,, 4—Arsenal ....Away
,, 29—Blackpool ....Home	,, 6—Cardiff City.........Away
Dec. 6—Chelsea ....Away	,, 11—Derby County ...Home
,, 13—Manchester U. ...Home	,, 18—Blackpool ....Away
,, 20—Preston N.E. ......Home	, 25—Chelsea ....Home
,, 25—Burnley ....Away	
,, 26—Burnley ....Home	May 2—Manchester U. ...Away

A copy of the league fixtures for the 1952/1953 season.

felt that they were giving our lads some stick. The guy in front of us turned around to ask us to curb our language – it was Bill Shankly! He didn't need to say a word, but just gave us a very stony look. We never said another thing throughout the remainder of the match. When the game was over, he did ask us how we were getting home, but we said that we had a lift organised. We got battered when we arrived home early the next morning. That was because we'd sagged school. But I think that it was probably more for causing so much worry to our parents.

Ronnie Bracegirdle

Ripped Off in Derby

We all went to Derby one day, six of us in a minibus going down to the Baseball Ground. We got there at ten o'clock in the morning. I never liked that ground, it always seemed to be waterlogged. We parked the van, had a stroll around to stretch our legs, and then dived into a little café for a late morning breakfast. Six full breakfasts and lashings of tea – mug after mug. It was now well after eleven o'clock, and there still wasn't a soul around. The guy in charge of the café casually said to us, 'What are you down for lads?' Well, in our red and white scarves and various other bits and pieces, I didn't think that there could be much room for confusion. After we told him, he informed us, again in a very casual manner, that the game had been called off sometime during the morning. It was obvious why he hadn't told us – those six breakfasts came to more than thirty quid! What a rip off. We were back in our own boozer before seven that night.

David Grooby

It Should Have Been Weetabix That Morning

One of the worst days I remember at Anfield was as a lad standing on the old Spion Kop with my mates. Two old friends had travelled over from Nelson in Lancashire to watch the Sheffield Wednesday match, when Liverpool played in the old First Division. They had arrived the night before and stayed at our house with their Mum and Dad, old friends of my parents. We had had our tea early so the olds could take the rest of the evening to soak up some refreshment and enjoy their meal, whilst we talked excitedly in our beds (well, sleeping bags) about the match we were about to witness. I had been to quite a few games before, but my mates, although avid supporters, had only been to one, and had never stood on the Kop.

    Saturday dawned, and we were all up as early as possible, racing about the house and generally wishing we were at Anfield. After a hasty breakfast, we went to the shops, where we were allowed a whole pound each to spend on sweets for the game, which was unheard of. Arriving home, we finally set off with scarves trailing out of the car window and in full voice. We got to Anfield and made our way through the customary crowds until we took up a not-too-crowded stance towards the back, where our dads could keep an eye on us but we thought we were far enough to join in all the

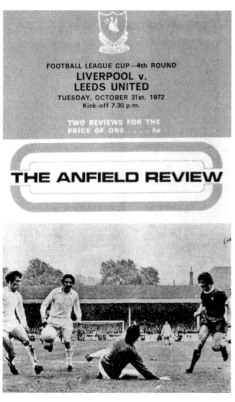

Above left: Match programme from Liverpool v Leeds United, Tuesday 31 October 1972.

Above right: Match programme from Liverpool v Queens Park Rangers, Saturday 20 December 1975.

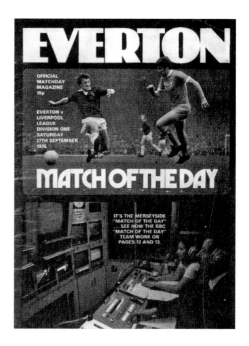

The official matchday magazine from Goodison, Saturday 27 September 1975, when, after a tough game, honours were even with a final score of 0-0.

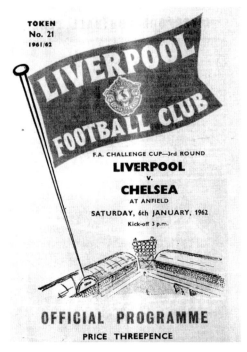

Above left: Match programme from Liverpool v Chelsea, Saturday 6 January 1962.

Above right: Match programme from Liverpool v Everton, Christmas Eve, 1949.

Tommy Laurence, Yeats and Lawler get the ball away.

songs with swearwords in. Kick-off came, and to be honest, the first half was pretty dull. During half-time we munched our sweets and made up tales about what would have happened if we were in the number eleven shirt. When the whistle went to signal the start of the second half, I was beginning to feel a little light-headed, which Dad put down to euphoria. Later on, in the special room underneath the ground reserved for the St John's ambulance (having fainted on the Kop), the medic put this down to malnutrition, or lack of breakfast, during which time I managed to miss two cracking goals in a 2-0 win for Liverpool, both scored at the Kop end. So always eat your Weetabix.

Jon Paul

For the Good of the Company

Ken loves going to the game, but he has to do it in a slightly different manner, there's all of the corporate seats business, none of this standing in the Kop anymore – the customers just wouldn't expect that type of treatment. He also gets quite a few invites himself, but you know what Ken's like for double scheduling! He sometimes gets tied up with other appointments and then asks me to do some of the corporate entertaining bit. I don't mind too much, although it means that I can't go to the game with my mates. What it does mean, however, is that I'm able to enjoy the game, have a few drinks and a good meal at Anfield, and, when it's all over, I get a cab, and we all get home in style – the things I do for the company!

Paul Stewart

For the Want of a Shoe

My mother was always very keen on the maxim that a teenage lad should have the right sized shoes to grow up with. So, instead of having half a size too big, my mother, being careful with her pennies, decided that she'd make sure that I had at least two sizes extra. In fact, at the age of seventeen with size 9-10 feet, I was walking around in size 13 shoes!

On the day in question, I was in my usual position right in the centre of the Kop – where all the action was. There was a particularly large crowd as we were playing against Leeds. Obviously, at that time, they were one of the top teams in the League. The crowd was terrific and the atmosphere was great. In order to see better I was standing with my heels on the step above – a common practice in the Kop. I was half leaning forward when Liverpool scored the first goal. Everyone, including me, leapt for joy, and my already loose, and now stretched, shoes were so stretched that one of them parted company with my feet! As the ground around was littered by all sorts of newspapers, dog ends, liquid matter and various other bits and pieces, the last thing that I wanted was to put my now be-socked foot down in this debris. For the next twenty-five minutes, in a particularly active period of play for Liverpool, I was hopping around on one leg. Going with the flow, I was being pushed up, down and across the

Kop, still standing on one foot, with my right leg growing increasingly more tired. When Liverpool scored their second goal and we all leapt into the air, I was so fatigued that I just had to put both feet on the ground. By the most amazing coincidence, my right foot landed in the shoe which I'd given up as lost almost half an hour earlier!

Trevor Burke

Martin's Disappeared

On our first date, my husband took me to the Kop. He carefully positioned me in front of a rail and between two burly dockers. Liverpool scored! The crowd surged forward and Martin disappeared. At the end of the game I waited for the crowds to leave, then made my way out. We'd come by car, and I stood like a waif and stray not even knowing which way the buses went to the Pier Head. After a few minutes Martin rushed up all concerned, he'd whipped into the pub on the corner of the Kop for a quick pint!

Jo Farrell

If You Can't Beat Them, Join Them

Saturday afternoon at Burnley is another memory. By now I'd adopted a policy of 'If you can't beat them, then join them'. In fact, I was beginning to enjoy going to the games and watching the football. Martin had driven over, but when we got there we couldn't find anywhere to park. By now it was getting very close to three o'clock. Suddenly, without any warning, Martin pulled the car to a stop, jumped out and shouted to me, 'You park the car and I'll see you after the game.' He then left me to it!

Jo Farrell

My One and Only Match

Many years ago I was taken to watch Liverpool play against Arsenal. I wasn't very impressed with the match, but I certainly liked looking at all of the floodlights. I don't really understand football. And even now, I can't for the life of me understand how grown men in the same family, living under the same roof, cannot both support the same team, but insist on having interminable arguments about the merits or otherwise of their respective teams. In our house, like many of the homes in the rest of Liverpool no doubt, the two teams in question are Liverpool and Everton.

Angela Parry

Who's in the Second Division?

On a Saturday evening, we would all huddle around the radio and listen to Sports Report at half-past five. Dad, an Evertonian, would sit there very quietly, not saying

Liverpool equalising against Sheffield Wednesday at Hillsborough.

The scene outside Wembley when the 'Dads and Lads' went for a day out from Liverpool.

One of our banners which goes everywhere with us.

a thing, that is until the announcer said, 'League Division Two', then my dad came into action, 'Who's in that division?' he would say, 'Barnsley, Doncaster, Scunthorpe, and guess who else?' He was just goading us and he'd do it every match, it used to really get to us. We still had a good side when we were in the Second Division. We had players like Geoff Twentyman, he was a tremendous player, and then we got Johnny Wheeler from Bolton he was an England international. It's got to be said that there was a feeling around Anfield at the time that everything wasn't right. We always seemed to be finishing third, and people were beginning to ask questions about whether we wanted to go into the First Division.

Gerry Tyrrell

Crushed Against the Crash Barrier

We were beating Arsenal 4-0, in our Championship-clinching match in the sixties. Ecstatic as always, I turned around to greet the Kop, only to be met by an on-rushing crowd. The next thing I knew was my back being pinned over the crash barrier. Unfortunately, although quite strong at the time, my back started bending ever further backwards over the bar. When the pain got really intense, I couldn't avoid screaming. Everybody was trying to hold off and pressing backwards. In the end when the pain had eased a little, I remember crawling out of the crowd and leaving ten minutes early – something which I never did. I had to walk to the Pier Head to try and straighten up.

Trevor Burke

The Voucher's Safe!

Another time, Martin and his brother took me to a 'special game'. The only special thing about it was that vouchers were being given out for a cup-tie. Once through the turnstiles they disappeared! I'd been lectured so much about keeping the voucher safe, that I stuffed it in my bra!

Jo Farrell

Two More Unemployed After That Arsenal Game

When I was working down South, I watched Liverpool on TV, playing in the last game of the '89 season. The people I was with, my company secretary and his wife, had joined me for dinner at my hotel. After the meal we settled down to watch the game. They didn't mind as they were both avid Arsenal supporters and they knew that I was fanatical about Liverpool. Arsenal were winning 1-0. I nipped out to the loo and when I got back they were dancing on the table – Arsenal had scored again! One thing led to another, as it so often does on this sort of occasion. The upshot was that at the end of the evening they were no longer in my employ. So, indirectly, Michael Thomas caused two people to join the ranks of the unemployed that night.

Ronnie Bracegirdle

The Milk Train Home

I soon got to know the times of trains returning from all over the country and taxied many supporters home in states of euphoria or despair. One night I waited for hours at Exchange Station. Crowds of supporters were coming out whenever a train arrived, but Martin and his mate weren't on any of them. Finally, one of the station staff came over to me and said, 'Sorry luv, but there are no more trains tonight. The next one will be coming into Lime Street.' My instructions from Martin had been very clear, 'Don't move.' I decided to stay put, which was just as well. Not very much later, Martin and his mate emerged from the station. They'd changed trains, gone for a quick pint, missed their train, and had to wait for the 'milk train'.

Jo Farrell

A Game to Remember

One Boxing Day, my father took me to Anfield and I always remember it was quite an experience because it was Liverpool v Manchester City. The most significant thing about this game was that the period we are talking about were war years when the Football League had been abandoned as such. At that time they used to have the North League and the South League and we would play teams like Crewe Alexandra, or we'd be playing Blackpool, or we'd be playing Notts County. All the players at that time were either on military service or in reserved occupations and one game of that particular period stands out a mile. The legendary Matt Busby was playing for Liverpool and guess who was in goal for Manchester City – none other than the great, and equally legendary, Frank Swift. Now Frank Swift was the England goalkeeper, he was killed, if you remember, in the Munich air crash. The other truly outstanding player on that day was Don Welsh, the Charlton player, who eventually became a manager of Liverpool. As I say, the game was played during the war, probably round about '44 or '45 – something of that nature anyway. As an impressionable young boy, eager to absorb and learn as many footballing skills as I could, the main point I can remember is when a free kick of some significance was taken. I'm not sure whether it was Don Welsh or Matt Busby, but obviously one or the other came to take that free kick. Rather than just take a normal free kick, they stepped over the ball, and the other fellow came up behind and rammed the ball into the back of the net. Now this was Frank Swift you know, and to be able to score against Frank Swift at the Kop end was par excellence. What a game!

Harold S. Scott

Alun Evans scoring against Manchester City.

CHAPTER 8

OTHER TIMES

Language!

The guy who sits behind us is a very nice guy, but he certainly knows how to use language. As soon as he's let forth with a mouthful, often about Benitez and the crazy way in which he manages the team, he taps me on the shoulder and apologises for using such bad language, but then, often less than a minute later, he'll be sounding off again – it's just the way he is!

Flo Johnston

The Americans are so Thick-Skinned

It wasn't that long after the Americans took over the ownership of the Club that most of us realised that they were only in it to make money. I think now that David Moores is aware of this, although I don't for one minute think that this was his opinion when he sold to them. They landed the club with a lot of debt due to the way that they financed the takeover. I don't know how the legal team could have been so blind. We have held many protests, including marches, but the Americans seem to be so thick-skinned that I don't believe that they'll sell until they're good and ready, and that means when they get an offer which they think is worth accepting. Meanwhile the club slips gently downhill. Goodness knows what will happen next season if one or two players do well in the World Cup!

James Bennett

The Lucky Injury

We had Larry Hughes playing centre half for us, and I can remember one game in particular that was at Anfield. In those days there were no substitutes allowed, and if you were injured and couldn't carry on, you went off. On this occasion Larry Hughes got injured and wasn't able to play properly, and I forget who it was that we were playing, but the thing about it was George Kay left Larry Hughes on the field. But what did he do, he moved him from centre half to centre forward, purely and simply for nuisance value. The ploy worked, and even better, at the very last kick of the game

Billy Liddell opens the first supporters' club in 1959.

Above left and right: Supporters demonstrations against the American's ownership of LFC.

Bob Paisley gets the freedom of the City of Liverpool, Wednesday 23 November 1983.

Larry Hughes slipped the ball over the goal line to score for Liverpool and we won that particular game. I always remember that because, you know, it had never been done before to leave an injured player on the field, with his bandage and everything else. I saw Larry Hughes about a month ago, in Saint John's Road in Waterloo, and I said to him, 'Do you ever remember that?' – he said 'Oh yes, I've still got the bandage!'

Harold S. Scott

The View from the Church Roof

The Charity Shield hasn't always been played at Wembley. In 1963 it was played between Everton and Liverpool at Goodison. Unfortunately, I didn't have a ticket, so I was walking around the outside of the ground trying to buy one, when I noticed some people standing on the roof of a nearby church. Another supporter, who obviously had the same idea as me, grabbed my arm, and for some unknown reason we ran into the church and sat down at the back. I seem to recall that there was a wedding taking place at the time.

Realising that there was no way up from inside the church, I went out of the church and along an alley which was just to the side. I climbed up a drainpipe and found myself on the lower roof. I edged my way up the roof, which was at an angle of about forty-five degrees, and then it was up another drainpipe onto the top roof. So far so good, but the top roof, to my horror, was pitched at a much steeper angle. The only

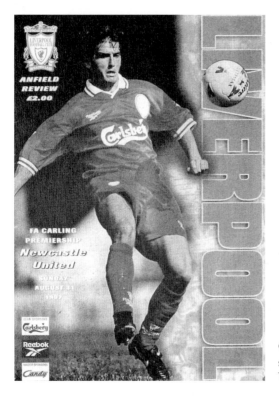

One of only two Liverpool programmes sold on the day of Diana, Princess of Wales's death.

option I was left with was to edge my way along the guttering onto an adjoining roof. Fortunately, I only weighed just over eight stone at the time, but it was a scary few minutes as I felt as though the guttering was about to give way at any minute. In the event, all I could see for my trouble was a tiny corner of the ground – it really hadn't been worth the effort.

John Sutherland

Where's the Ring?

It is always a great pleasure to be asked to be the Best Man of a lifelong friend. I had the honour on 10 April 1982 to be the Best Man at the wedding of Ray and Brenda Plested. The day, however, was a Saturday, and the 'kickoff' was at 3 o'clock – it couldn't have been a worse time as far as I was concerned. Liverpool were due to play away to Manchester City. There was only one solution to the problem, and that was to use a transistor radio with one of those small earphones which look like hearing aids. I thought that I'd be able to feed the wire under my shirt and out of the back of the collar. All went to plan, I even bought new Duracell batteries to ensure that there was no risk of fading. Also, I didn't get my hair cut for weeks, so that the wire coming out of the collar would be hidden. The service started, and the vicar was prattling on when there was a news flash from Maine Road. I pressed the earphone harder into my ear to hear the news that Liverpool had scored. I was straining desperately to hear the

Liverpool conceding a dramatic goal against Sheffield United.

details of the scorer when Ray poked me and gave me a quizzical look. The vicar was staring, and even Brenda craned her head to see what was going on. Unfortunately, I'd missed the point where I was supposed to hand over the ring! All was well however, the ring was duly placed on her finger, Liverpool scored five, and all-in-all, it was an unforgettable day.

David Pennington

Tragedy in Success

Liverpool were in the Second Division, the gates were small, and Bill Shankly had recently joined the club. In the year I'm talking about Liverpool won the Second Division championship – I think it was the 1961/62 season, and they went up to the First Division. That was the old First Division, well before today's Premier League. There was no technology around the ground or in offices, everything in the ticket office was done manually. Liverpool, who were beginning to be successful, were in cup matches and other matches, and Jimmy McInnes, who was the club secretary, was overwhelmed with the volume of work. He only got an extra couple of girls in the office, and they just couldn't deal with the sheer volume. There were no systems and very little organisation. He was an awfully nice man, a very quiet man, but he just couldn't cope with the intense pressure. One day, when everything was getting on top of him, he just went down to the Kop end and went into a turnstile and hung himself in the turnstile. That was a very tragic event and in the first year that they were in the First Division.

Ken Davies

The Brazilians in Japan

We went to Japan in 1981 to watch Liverpool against Flamengo. It was a Sunday game in the middle of the afternoon. There was only about eleven of us in the excursion, and six of them won it from the Echo or Radio City. One lad had a loan on his Access – he might just be getting to the end of his loan repayments now! Before we got to Japan, we had a few days in Hong Kong. But the guy who'd got the loan wasn't interested in Hong Kong, he wasn't even interested in Japan – his only interest was the match. We got to the stadium about two hours before kick-off. Fortunately I'd brought my hunting horn, so that signalled to everyone that the British contingent were present. When we arrived the Brazilians were warming up – Liverpool weren't! It was freezing cold in the middle of December, and the pitch was rock hard. When the teams came out, Neal, who was leading them out, had the ball in his hands. When he reached the pitch, he gave it the normal bounce just as you do. The ball rebounded over his head, obviously unexpectedly, because he didn't think that the pitch was as hard as it was. He then put his hands on the pitch and looked round as if to say 'Bloody hell, this is hard isn't it?' Before we'd been playing for half an hour we were losing 3-0, we were getting absolutely battered, but at least we were having a go. The lad who had had the loan on his Access just put his head in his hands. I said to him, 'Never mind, we might equalise in the second half.' He became a little bit abusive towards me! 'Don't be bloody stupid, we're getting battered, this is the end of my life', sort of thing. I felt really sorry for him. Luckily enough, the Brazilians eased up in the second half, they let us into it a little bit and we held them to 3-0. On the morning of the match the manager of the Brazilians had announced that unless his team won 5-0 or more, then it would be a lousy result for Flamengo. That was worrying, but the Brazilian manager was right, they were far, far superior to us. That was the first season that we had Mr Grobbelaar in goal, and he pulled off some tremendous saves in the second half – only for him the floodgates might have been well and truly opened. With all the internationals in their team, it was almost like playing the Brazilian national side – we didn't have much of a chance against them, but it was a good experience to go!

David Pennington

Please Don't Punch My Lights Out, I'm Only Small

We were at Villa Park in the Semi-final of the League Cup, and I'd be about thirteen or fourteen at the time. I was very small, so Keith had a little footstool made for me to stand on during the game. We went down with George, and another chap who used to work in the shop, Aldi. The bloke on the turnstile didn't want us to take the stool into

Christmas is always a good time
for young Liverpool supporters.

the ground, but we persuaded him. A few of us ended up standing on the stool, as it
allowed us to get a really good view of the match. There were some people behind us
who objected, and threatened to 'punch my lights out' – they didn't!

David Lennon

Never Say Dye!

In 1950 we played Arsenal in the FA Cup Final at Wembley, but the first round that
we'd played in that year was against Blackburn Rovers. We'd drawn at Blackburn 0-0
and then they came back to Anfield the following Wednesday afternoon for the replay.
The game was played in the afternoon, as this was long before the time of floodlights,
of course. We'd got our money to go, but when we got there we couldn't get in – it was
chocka! Lots of adults had climbed into the boy's pen. There was nothing else to do but
to make our way home. On the way, me and my brother Eddy decided to buy some red
and white hats to show our support, but first we decided to try and get the results from

the Echo offices, which at that time were in Victoria Street. This wasn't too far away from where we lived in the centre of town, and it was the best way to get the results. As the scores came in, the printers used to shout down to the people waiting below. Anyway, there we were in these paper hats walking through the centre of town, and it started raining. Before long the dye from the hats had come out, and was running in little rivulets down our faces. Mum wasn't too pleased when we arrived home, as by now our shirts too were full of the red dye. Try as she did, Mum just couldn't get it out, so we couldn't go to school for a few days after that!

Gerry Tyrrell

What Might Have Been!

As a schoolboy, and growing up in Kirkby, a suburb of Liverpool, I thought very little about anything other than soccer. I am therefore, to this day, still amazed how I ever managed to get an education and end up with a degree. Well, I guess that must be a testament to the UK education system! Whenever I was asked by anyone what I wanted to be when I grew up, the reply was always 'I want to be a [professional] footballer and play for Everton!' Yes – Everton – since that was the team that my father supported when I first became interested in soccer.

I can honestly say the best football I ever played was between the ages of eleven and fifteen for the school [Brookfield] team, which was run by a marvellous motivator and disciplinarian Mr Des Hughes, and following that for the Kirkby Boys' team. Mr Hughes, being a rugby player himself, worked miracles with our team by introducing, for example, England training methods, twice a week, and a system of incentives and disincentives to perform better. He built a 'world-beating team' and we were dubbed 'The Brookfield Babes', after the great 'Busby Babes', by the Liverpool Echo. The team was very successful between 1961 and 1963, played fifty games without defeat and scored 225 goals with only 23 against.

The following season, however, we were unceremoniously kicked out the Liverpool League! The reason given was that our school, the first purpose-built comprehensive school in England, was too big compared to the other schools in Liverpool; the real reason, we suspected, was that our rivals couldn't take our domination of the league and cup competitions and wanted us out!

The next year I was fourteen and played for Kirkby Boys, the same year that the great Joe Royle played for Liverpool Boys at centre forward. He was a Goliath of a player even then. However, they say that the bigger they are, the harder they fall, and a memorable moment for me was when I delivered a scything slide tackle on him and sent him flying. It was great!

We met Liverpool Boys in the final of two competitions that year, in the Dimmer Cup and the Lancashire Schools Trophy. Both of the finals were two-legged affairs with Liverpool winning three of the four legs and taking the silverware! Mind you if they hadn't have had big Joe spearheading the line-up I think things would have been different!

It was after one of those games for Kirkby Boys that three players of our team, including myself, were approached by a Liverpool scout. Kevin Marsh and Phil Toumey were asked to sign as apprentice professionals and I went to Melwood as an amateur player. I quickly found out one of Liverpool FC's secrets of success – fitness! At the start of a new season it was four weeks before we were allowed to kick a ball! It was running, running and more running. A short time later, during a training session, I was introduced to the infamous sweat box which consisted of four vertically mounted boards the area of a goal mouth, placed in a square formation such that there was about eight metres between opposite sides of the square. Three minutes in the 'box' and you'd had it! Basically two players stand in the middle of the square. The first player hits the ball hard onto a side of the square. The second player has to control the rebounding ball and deliver a shot to another side, and so on. It is not hard to imagine the amount of stopping, controlling, turning and shooting that goes on in a three-minute period. It was knackering!

It was after one such session that I was pulled out of training and sent to play in a game being played in another area of the training ground. When I got closer to the players I noticed it was a game between the newly installed apprentice professionals. Another thing I noticed was that watching the game was 'The Boss'. Shanks was eyeing the new talent that had arrived at Liverpool and I was to play in front of him.

Needless to say I was nervous, as was everyone else. The great man had such presence and aura you couldn't help but be fearful of him. Nobody played well in that game but it was not for want of trying. There is a saying that if you want to play for Liverpool you have to be prepared to run through a brick wall backwards. That game in particular, as in many more amateur games to come for Liverpool, was to typify that saying!

The chief trainer of the amateurs was Reuben Bennett, an ex-professional goalkeeper from the Scottish League. By contrast to the complex motivational methods of my school team coach, the methods adopted by Reuben Bennett were, to say the least, primitive. He dished out discipline with a fervour bordering on nastiness. There would never be a good word for anyone, just criticism. I remember a talented goalkeeper, who was subjected to endless shots at goal one after the other for fifteen minutes. Reduced to tears at his incessant criticism and badgering, the totally exhausted and weeping goalkeeper told our Reuben were to get off and left the grounds for good. I must confess to being close to tears on more than one occasion myself at the hands of Reuben. However, one man's meat is another man's poison and some players responded to his regime. Reuben Bennett's approach did not detract, however, from the superb training methods which were part of the Liverpool trademark.

During my two years as an amateur for Liverpool I saw some make it to becoming professional. I remember one time in the bath after training discussing the game with the lads when Ted 'Jock' McDougall came in to announce that he had been offered professional terms. We were all green with envy of course and wanted to know what he was to do. The trouble was that he was in his last year as an apprentice printer, which in those days was a highly respected and high paying trade. Eventually Jock, a prolific goal scorer, made the right decision, and forsaking his indentures for his boots, joined the ranks of many a top class team during his career.

My regular training buddy for a time was Brian Hall. He was studying for a degree at Preston University and did not want to sign terms until he had graduated. Brian and I used to give it all we had at training sessions, it was just that Brian had a bit more to give than me and was always that yard quicker! I remember one Saturday I was down for the first time as reserve for the 'A' team against Everton at Bellfield training ground. The derby games were, of course, the best games of the year, and I wasn't looking forward to sitting it out on the bench. Brian was late as he had to travel from Preston by train and bus and was held up in traffic. I was told to get ready – and the adrenalin started pumping. Just as we were about to go out onto the pitch however, in came the red-faced Brian to steal away my debut game for the 'A' Team. I think he felt a bit sorry for me as I didn't look too pleased! Brian went on to finish his degree and, of course, the rest is history as they say.

Douggie Livermore, who is a year my junior, also attended Brookfield and was keeping up the record of Kirkby lads being chosen to play for Liverpool. It should be noted, that in case the reader thinks otherwise, hundreds of players from all over the UK are invited to play in the amateur ranks each year. Unfortunately, only a few make it into the top grades. It is, of course, just that dream that keeps you going. Douggie was a slight, small lad when he arrived and was always being caught in possession with the ball. Some years later he was almost unrecognisable as he filled out the famous red jersey – a testament to the training he received from the club and of course the hard work put in by Douggie himself.

I enjoyed my time at Liverpool as a footballing experience and for the camaraderie with the other guys, but I can't say that I really enjoyed my football. Perhaps it was the ulterior motive of becoming a footballer – a pro – that detracted from the true spirit of soccer: the simple enjoyment of just playing the game for its own sake. No, for me it has to be as an eleven-year-old sitting in the middle of a big puddle in the pouring rain, clutching my first schoolboy medal after winning one of the most enjoyable games of my life.

As I reach fifty, and having finally hung up my boots at the age of forty-five, I can look back on forty years of playing and watching this great game, a game that has provided me with immense excitement and pleasure, and I am very proud to say the Liverpool FC has played a big part in all of it.

Ian Durant
Kuala Lumpur

The Old Lady's Brolly

One Saturday afternoon, it was time for me to take my turn and act as the dutiful husband – my wife had insisted that I accompanied her on a shopping trip to Southport; Liverpool were playing a difficult league game at Anfield. As it wouldn't be worth mentioning this important fact to my wife, I decided to take alternative action and install an earphone – no major problems were foreseen. Suddenly, just as we were walking past Woolworth's, the news came through of a Liverpool goal. Instinctively, I jumped and yelled 'Yes!' It's always difficult to control the volume of the shout, especially when wearing the earphone. The sudden scream startled a little old lady walking by the side of us. In fact, it startled her so much that she raised her rolled umbrella to hit me. Fortunately I was too quick for her, and a neat body swerve ensured my escape.

David Pennington

The Ticket Feud

I think probably the one game that I've seen in all my years that I remember every single ball kicked, would be the same that nine out of ten supporters would give you, and that would be the '65 Cup Final, when, to me, St John scored the finest goal anybody has ever scored at Wembley. Nobody could beat that goal, because that goal was the one that won the Cup and that was the one that was important. The background to the game is that, where I lived in Edge Hill, there was a pub on every corner and most nights, five or six nights a week, I used to say to my dad, 'Do you fancy a pint?' Before I knew it, his coat was on, and he was halfway down the road to the pub. Anyway, all the regulars in the pub were people that he'd known since he was at school, they were all his school friends. One night we were down at the pub – it was just before the tickets were given out for the '65 Cup Final. Liverpool announced that they'd been given the customary 10,000 tickets, which was all that they got in those days, and that seven out of ten season ticket holders would get a ticket. The rest, together with the people who stood on the Kop, would be entered into a draw, and every third ticket would qualify for a Cup Final ticket – I was lucky! I was the one. So I went down and paid seven and six for a Cup Final ticket, unbelievable now. So I went into the pub, and I was showing everybody this ticket – I'm going to Wembley! And a guy named Jimmy Barr, who was a taxi driver and a friend of my father, said to me 'That's my ticket! I'm a season ticket holder, and they've got my money before the ball is kicked'. So I said, 'It's not my fault Jim. If I could get a season ticket I'd get one'. The whole thing went very sour, it was silly. Jimmy Barr was adamant that I should give him the ticket, and I'm clutching the ticket saying 'Come on Jim, this is my bloody ticket, I queued up, I drew the lucky number'. And from that day, to the day he died that man never spoke to me again, because I had his Cup Final ticket!

Alan Reason

I Went to the Wedding on My Own

Some time before we were married, we'd both been invited to the evening 'do' of my friend's wedding. It was Derby day in 1984, 20 October, and we'd both been to the game, at opposite ends you understand! For a change, Everton had won by the odd goal. After the game I made my way to Paul's house, but he wasn't in. So I went down to his favourite pub, but he wasn't there either. After going back to his house once more, I decided to go to the wedding on my own. Next day, when I eventually did track him down, he confessed to me that he didn't know what my reaction would be when I saw him after the match. He'd decided to 'go to ground', and ended up in the Pineapple, a pub which he never frequented.

Margo Stewart

Decimalisation

What did I do about decimalisation? Well, I got the use of the Three Hundred Club for the evening, and I turned the whole business into a social event. I got cardboard money, and I got all the staff in and we played bingo. The bar was open, and I had sandwiches for all the catering staff. They took it in turn, sometimes they would be sitting at the tables, and at other times they would be serving behind the counters. Staff had to come up and buy their tea and meat pies and use the new money. Instead of giving in half a crown or one and six, and they had to see if they could get it right in pounds and pence. Also, the people who were acting as cashiers or sales staff had to give the right change in the new money. We did this for a couple of weeks, so when decimalisation came around, all the women that served on the football ground had been trained. I'd never got any direction to do that, it was just that catering was my responsibility, so I never asked anybody whether I could do it, or give the girls free sandwiches and a bingo night on the club, I just did it. It was good fun – they wanted it to continue! In those days we had over a hundred staff around the ground, so we couldn't afford to pay extra wages. They had to come in to learn.

Ken Davies

A Long Weekend Without Food

We weren't often beaten at Anfield, but on this particular occasion we were – I can't even remember who we were playing. I used to get a shilling a week pocket money at that time, so I walked to the ground, I paid nine pence to get in, three pence for the programme, and then walked home. And that was whether it was rain, sleet, snow, it didn't matter – Saturday was football. So that was my pocket money committed. On this particular day, when I got home, my father said to me 'How did the game go?', so I said 'We got beat', and he started laughing. He just read about the games in the Echo, he didn't go to football matches any more. It was me who was the fanatic, so he probably just put up with it. He then said something like 'Oh, they're bloody rubbish that team, I don't know why you waste your pocket money on them'. Then it all degenerated, and I said 'I'm going to bed', and this was like half-past six, seven o'clock on a Saturday night. So he said 'What about your tea?' and I said 'I'll come down after if you leave me alone'. So there I was in bed – it was only a two-up, two-down house – and I could hear my dad saying to my mother, 'You'd better call him down for his tea'. And she said, 'No, if he's not at the table, then he doesn't eat.' So time went on, and it came up again, and she said, 'I'm telling you, if he comes down then he eats, and if he doesn't come down, then he's not hungry'. I didn't get out of bed 'till Monday morning to go to work. I never got out of bed, because my mum said 'That's it. If you can't sit down at the table, then that's it'. And I wasn't going to sit down at the table because I knew that I would be the butt of all the jokes all over again, so I stayed in bed!

Alan Reason